THE ECONOMISTS' DIET

THE SURPRISING FORMULA
FOR LOSING WEIGHT
AND KEEPING IT OFF

CHRISTOPHER PAYNE, PhD, and ROB BARNETT

TOUCHSTONE

New York   London   Toronto   Sydney   New Delhi

Touchstone
An Imprint of Simon & Schuster, Inc.
1230 Avenue of the Americas
New York, NY 10020

First Touchstone hardcover edition January 2018

TOUCHSTONE and colophon are registered trademarks
of Simon & Schuster, Inc.

For information about special discounts for bulk purchases,
please contact Simon & Schuster Special Sales at 1-866-506-1949
or business@simonandschuster.com.

The Simon & Schuster Speakers Bureau can bring authors to your live event.
For more information or to book an event,
contact the Simon & Schuster Speakers Bureau
at 1-866-248-3049 or visit our website at www.simonspeakers.com.

Manufactured in the United States of America

1   3   5   7   9   10   8   6   4   2

Library of Congress Cataloging-in-Publication Data

Names: Payne, Christopher, author. | Barnett, Rob (Robert Andrew), 1978– author.
Title: The economists' diet : the surprising formula for losing weight and keeping it off / by Christopher Payne, Ph.D. and Rob Barnett.
Description: New York : Touchstone, 2018.
Identifiers: LCCN 2017021827 (print) | LCCN 2017031617 (ebook) |
9781501160714 (paperback)
Subjects: LCSH: Reducing diets—Popular works. | Weight loss—Psychological aspects—Popular works. | BISAC: HEALTH & FITNESS / Weight Loss. | HEALTH & FITNESS / Healthy Living. | BUSINESS & ECONOMICS / Economics / Theory.
Classification: LCC RM222.2 (ebook) | LCC RM222.2 .P393 2018 (print) |
DDC 613.2/5—dc23
LC record available at https://lccn.loc.gov/2017021827

ISBN 978-1-5011-6070-7
ISBN 978-1-5011-6072-1 (ebook)

For my family, with all my love:
Nadia, who has been an endless source
of motivation and inspiration,
and our children,
Faris, Hala, and Cyrus.
—C.P.

To my beloved wife, Anne Marie,
and our children, George and Ramona.
—R.B.

CONTENTS

THE
ECONOMISTS'
DIET

INTRODUCTION

When most people think about economics, they think about interest rates, business planning, or talking heads commenting on monetary policy. But it's much more than that: it's a science of human decision making that can help you make better food choices and achieve lasting weight loss. As two successful dieters who also happen to be professional economists, we know that key economic principles underpin a set of easy-to-understand behavioral best practices—which we call *microhabits*—that will enable you to eat less in a world of constant temptation.

Of course, we expect that to many, the claim that economics provides the solution to our weight gain and obesity epidemic will come as a surprise. But it shouldn't: after all, economics explains why so many people overeat in the first place. As food has become less expensive and more plentiful in the past half century, it's become easier to consume more of it. With fewer budgetary constraints to keep our all-too-regular desires to eat in check, the result is an ever-increasing rate of people classified as obese or overweight.

1

INTRODUCTION

In this environment, it's no wonder that so many hopeful dieters become frustrated. For all the information out there about how to lose weight, dieting remains a seemingly unwinnable battle fought against a tsunami of cheap and abundant food. Thousands of books and articles have been written on the subject, and yet 70 percent of Americans are still either overweight or obese. You know the difference between good food and bad food. You know that you are eating and drinking more than you should. You know to avoid burgers and fries in favor of leafy greens and other veggies. You know what to do, but you still don't do it.

And that's exactly why we felt compelled to write this book and share with you our core message: losing weight and keeping it off are far more about behavior than nutrition.

This is, as you have no doubt figured out already, a different kind of diet book. We aren't going to delve into the science of weight gain or provide strict meal plans that you must follow if you have any prayer of losing a pound. We're not going to tell you that you should become a vegan or go on a juice cleanse or cut out all foods except kale and coconut water. We are not going to do this because you have likely heard it all before, and yet you're still here. We were there, too. As of January 2018, we have, between us, eighteen years of experience with successful weight loss. Chris lost forty-five pounds over an eighteen-month period starting in 2004 and is, as he writes this, fifty-five pounds below his highest weight.

INTRODUCTION

Starting in 2014, Rob lost seventy-five pounds over a similar period and has successfully maintained his weight loss ever since. We might not be nutrition experts, but through our experience, we have developed what we believe is the most pragmatic and effective approach to losing weight, one that you won't find in any other book.

And while you might assume that a diet plan rooted in the principles of economics would favor a lot of jargon or complex analyses, our diet plan is actually quite simple. The plain fact of the matter is that people gain weight by doing one thing and one thing only: eating too much food. While a few rare and incredibly fortunate people may be genetically inclined toward being thin, most slim people aren't inherently different from fat people; they are thin because they behave differently. This is obvious from looking at data and trends; we also know it to be true from personal experience.

We, Rob and Chris, met while working at Bloomberg, a leading financial software, data, and media company. We were based in their Washington, DC, office, and our roles involved analyzing the business impact of government actions and regulations. Our careers and related lifestyles presented the same obstacles to healthy living that so many people face today: long days, endless stress, indulgent dinners, and an ample supply of cheap snacks. Outside of work, short of time but with plenty of disposable income, we chose to enjoy ourselves by frequently eating out and eating too much. In the process, we both went from normal to overweight and ended up clinically obese; in Rob's case, severely obese. When we finally embarked on our own weight loss journeys, we recognized that we had neither the time nor the inclination to achieve the perfect bodybuilder physique; we just wanted to be healthy again.

We were once fat, but now we're not. It hasn't been easy, but losing weight has helped us feel happier, healthier, and generally better, and now we want to share our stories and know-how with you. We hope that by telling you our unique approach to weight loss, you will be able to shed your own poundage and keep it off for good. As you will discover, we are not interested in quick fixes or crash diets that help you to lose weight quickly only to gain it all back once you stop following the program. Extreme diets may sound good, but they are—as you probably already know from having tried them—difficult, if not impossible, to follow over the long term. In short, they are unsustainable.

Instead, what we provide in the pages that follow will enable you to make long-term improvements to your health by developing new microhabits to ensure dieting success for the rest of your life. If you are obese like we were, getting rid of those extra pounds could take eighteen months or more. For the average American, who is twenty-three pounds heavier than his or her desired weight,[1] you're looking at a diet taking at least six months. Either way, once you've lost the weight, you will have adopted a whole new approach to food: one that allows you to enjoy eating without all the stress of crash dieting.

Rather than subscribing to a particular food plan or program, we lost weight by applying what we know best—economics—to our waistlines. By carefully considering economic theories, real-world data, and our own personal experiences, we developed behavioral best practices that helped us control our impulses to overeat as well as approach food in a healthier way. For example, we think it's time to abandon the idea of eating three square meals a day; and we strongly advocate weighing yourself at the start of each day, for reasons that we'll soon explain.

Although this book is rooted in economics, we want to emphasize that this is not a theoretical guide to weight loss. It is a practical guide written by two individuals who have achieved lasting weight loss results. We designed the Economists' Diet so that anyone can follow it, whether you have a PhD or barely understand the difference between supply and demand.

We know that losing weight is hard, because we've done it. And we know that keeping the weight off can often feel even harder. But we also know that it is possible and that the results are worth the effort. We hope that by reading this book, you will look at weight loss in a whole new light, and by applying our insights and advice to your own life, you will be able to make better decisions, form new habits, and achieve a healthier lifestyle for years to come.

We are rooting for you. If we can do it, so can you.

INTRODUCTION

Fat and not particularly happy about it.

Fall 2003
220 pounds

Fall 2013
250 pounds

Feeling much happier about our weight and our health.

Winter 2007/8
174 pounds

Summer 2017
175 pounds

INTRODUCTION

HOW WE GOT FAT

Before we launch into the practical elements of this book, we thought it would be helpful to share a little bit of our backstories so that you know how we arrived at the ideas we're about to put forth. We also hope you can draw some inspiration from our success stories that will motivate you as you begin your weight loss journey.

We'll start with Chris.

Chris's Story

As of this writing, I, Chris, am forty-four years old and have maintained a healthy weight for more than ten years. Prior to losing forty-five pounds over a period of roughly eighteen months, I spent most of my adult life overweight (at times obese) and unhappy about it.

Even as a child growing up in Croydon, a suburb of London, I was aware that my weight was a problem. When I was about ten years old, my school conducted a survey of each student's weight, and I was the heaviest person in the class. It didn't really bother me that much at the time—I just knew I was bigger than my classmates.

That all changed a few years later, when, as a young teenager, I was subjected to name calling by some of my peers. This made me more self-conscious about my weight. Like an increasing number of children today,[2] I experimented with dieting, using SlimFast, a fad diet featuring meal replacements that was popular at the time and consists mostly of drinking flavored canned protein shakes. I had some success, but as with all quick fixes, it didn't last long.

As an older teen, I would go out with friends so often that I sometimes quite literally forgot to eat. I can't say for certain, but I'm pretty sure that I was the lightest I've ever been in my adult life around this time. I certainly wasn't thin, but I wasn't overweight, either.

Three months after I started at university, living away from home for the first time in my life, a friend pointed out to me that I had gained a lot of weight, likely from eating copious amounts of fried food washed down with many pints of Guinness stout. Actually, he told me that I was "looking fat." (A really good friend, that guy.) In addition, I started to notice a bunch of red marks on my stomach and under my arms. Not knowing what these were and fearing the worst (I'm a bit of a hypochondriac), I went to the doctor, who tested me for a couple of rare disorders. When the tests came back negative, he concluded there could be only one explanation: stretch marks. At the time, I didn't really appreciate the lesson here; it's quite remarkable how much weight you can gain in a short amount of time if you really go for it.

I was officially fat, but I still didn't do anything about it until my final year of school, when, in addition to preparing for my year-end exams, I tried the SlimFast diet again.

As before, it worked for a time, but I eventually regained all the weight I had lost (and then some).

After finishing school, I took a job in the financial district of London—what locals refer to as the "City" because it covers the square mile of the original Roman city of Londinium. The City is basically the Wall Street of the United Kingdom, and the lifestyle is pretty much the same.

First as an investor and later as a stockbroker, I was taken out to eat and drink a lot and did a lot of client entertaining myself. There were many enormous business lunches and regular business trips during which I would gorge on airport food only to be treated to yet another large meal upon arriving at my destination. Don't get me wrong: the food was excellent (except for the airport stuff, of course). But as you can imagine, it wasn't all that excellent for my waistline.

At this stage, it may be helpful to put some numbers on all of this. I am five foot ten inches tall. I am guessing that right before I started university, when I was at my lightest, I weighed around 160 to 165 pounds. Three months and many stretch marks later, I was closing in on 190 pounds. When I left university, after my second attempt at the SlimFast diet, I think I may have been back down to around 180 pounds. But then I began a steady climb back up the scale.

I should stress that it wasn't just the entertaining that caused me to gain weight. I simply ate too much all of the time. Why? Because I was bored, frustrated, and depressed in my job. Every day, the alarm clock went off at 5:42 a.m. on the dot. I got up, showered, shaved, got dressed, and was out the door at 6:03. I took the 6:18 train and got to my desk by 6:50. The daily team meeting began at 7:00, after which I would eat a large breakfast and begin calling clients. My first call started at 8:30, and generally I was busy until 11:00 or 11:30, by which time I was tired and fed up. Selling stocks is a pretty miserable profession—at least it was for me and most, if not all, of my colleagues. Admittedly, stockbrokers are some of the best paid salesmen in the world, but making those daily calls to clients is painful.

But there was more to it than that. Picking or recommending the right investments—for example, stocks that do better than the Dow Jones or the Standard & Poor's (S&P) 500—is almost impossible. Of course, the laws of probability mean that some investors will "beat" the market; and those that do inevitably attribute their success to their own intrinsic genius. But in all my years of experience, I never encountered anyone who convinced me that his or her investment performance was anything other than random—sometimes good, sometimes bad. And this is hardly surprising: in a world racked by uncertainty, there's simply no way to predict what will happen next.

How did all of this contribute to my obesity? Because, even though I was no more capable than anyone else of picking the right stocks, I was different in one key way: I was honest with myself. I *knew* that I would never be able to beat the market and that my career was failing to give me the mental stimulation and satisfaction that I needed.

To sum it up, I was bored, and I found that the best way to comfort and distract myself was to go out for nice, large lunches with my friends. Three friends in particular—Tim, Alun, and Omar—worked near my office, so the four of us would meet regularly to complain about work and life in general. As I tucked into my meal, my bulging belly was the last thing on my mind.

One of my favorite lunches was lasagna and fries—the big, thick heavy ones, oozing grease, which we Brits call chips. It doesn't take a nutritional genius to realize that this is a bad lunch from a health perspective, although it was quite satisfying from a drown-your-sorrows-in-carbs perspective. When I combined these lunches with a grande white chocolate mocha from Starbucks and an afternoon watching the clock, the weight soon stacked up.

Of course, my gluttony did not end when I left the office. After an unsatisfying day at work, the last thing I wanted to do was go home, exercise, and eat a sensible dinner. Many days in the City would end with me at the pub, bemoaning work yet again. Once home, I'd eat a full dinner: perhaps another round of pasta or a premade microwave meal or delivery from one of the multiple restaurants near my home. As the pounds added up, I knew I needed to do something about it, but I had no real motivation to change my ways.

Occasionally, I would discuss the problem with my

brother, Richard, who has, at times, suffered from the same weight issues as me. But the discussion was always lighthearted and often conducted over yet another large lunch. Richard and I preferred to meet at McDonald's, where my standard order was a supersized Big Mac and fries followed by a cheeseburger for dessert. You read that right: I literally ate a cheeseburger for dessert. The extra burger helped prolong the lunch so I could buy myself a few more precious minutes away from the office.

My diet of excess and abundance finally culminated on Sunday, January 4, 2004. I had taken off Christmas and New Year's Day, so this was my last night of holiday vacation before I had to return to work. For me, January 5, 2004, signified the beginning of what was sure to be yet another personally unsatisfying year. To make myself feel better, I stuffed myself with my favorite Indian dishes: chicken vindaloo, pilau rice, naan bread, and the vegetable dish saag aloo accompanied by multiple crisp papadums. I knew instinctively that after a gluttonous Christmas, this was the final straw for my body. I was fat, unhappy, and, to quote the British black comedy (and one of my favorite movies) *Withnail and I*, "making an enemy of my own future."

The following morning, I did something that I very rarely did in those days: I stood on the scale. And to my chagrin, I discovered that I was obese. At 220 pounds, I was disgusted with myself. To this day, I don't really know what changed in my brain, but I knew something had to be done. The Economists' Diet had begun.

INTRODUCTION

Rob's Story

My story is similar to Chris's, but without quite so much work-related nihilism.

Although America's obesity epidemic was on the rise in the late 1970s and early 1980s, I, Rob, wasn't particularly fat as a child, though people may have described me as "husky" or "full framed."

Looking back, I believe my childhood eating habits were probably conducive toward a healthy weight. My parents were frugal, which meant that we ate most meals at home (a fact that, as we'll explain later in this book, greatly reduces the risk of overeating). My mother was also not a pushover, and whatever she had prepared was the only thing on offer for us to eat. If she made a broccoli and rice casserole, my sister and I had to eat broccoli and rice casserole or nothing at all.

Mom rarely cooked dishes from scratch, but she still sought balance. My mother's idea of preparing meals epitomized the American ideal of convenience cooking: mixing and matching ingredients from various boxes, cans, and packages to design a quick and easy meal. Think Hamburger Helper with a side of frozen broccoli. Or chicken casserole made from cubed chicken, a can of Campbell's cream of mushroom soup, and some Town House crackers sprinkled on top. By today's nutritional standards, these meals might not be considered that healthy, but they were simple and served in limited amounts, meaning that I wasn't overeating.

My family typically ate out once or twice a week. As a reward for sitting quietly through the weekly sermon at the United Methodist Church in Simpsonville, South Carolina, my parents would treat us to brunch at our local Tex-Mex restaurant. To this day, I still greatly enjoy Tex-Mex food; I also still require a good bribe to get me to attend church. Other restaurant visits were reserved for evenings when Mom needed a reprieve from her daily duties. We almost always went to "family style" places such as Shoney's or Ryan's Steak House, where you could order a "meat and three": a serving of meat and three side dishes. My sister and I would have preferred more trips to McDonald's, but fast-food restaurants were limited almost exclusively to road trips.

Off at college, I'm almost certain I gained the so-called freshman fifteen like everybody else, though it's hard to say for sure because I didn't weigh myself frequently. I'm five foot ten, so, while an extra fifteen pounds was certainly not great, I carried it well enough that it wasn't too noticeable. Generally, alcohol and pot aside, my lifestyle choices in college trended toward healthy. I had plenty of free time, so I exercised almost daily at the local recreation center. For food, I had a meal plan at the school cafeteria during most of my undergraduate program, and my mother would have been proud of how frequently I elected to eat salad.

Good habits don't necessarily last forever, though, and they're highly influenced by one's environment. I don't want to blame my wife and children for my eventual weight gain, but things definitely went downhill after I finished grad school, got a full-time job, married, had children, and, most notably, moved to Washington, DC.

Of those things, getting a full-time job, and thus having more money to spend, was probably the biggest reason I started to gain weight. In grad school, I had a tight budget and often had to make tough choices: Would I rather have a burrito from Boca Grande or a couple of Pabst Blue Ribbons at the Model Café? It was probably healthier weightwise to choose the beers, which I did often.

Once you've entered the work world, you discover quickly that eating out occasionally is one luxury that most people can afford. I couldn't afford the fanciest apartment or the fanciest car, but I could certainly pay to have someone else cook dinner for me once in a while. After my wife, Anne Marie, and I secured jobs in Boston, dining out became the norm.

We moved into a small apartment in Boston's Back Bay neighborhood. We didn't have much space, but we did have access to some of the city's best eateries and bars. The proprietors of Crossroads Irish Pub, the Eastern Standard, and a handful of other local establishments knew us by name. I also bought my lunch most days—

because I could. My behavior was ultimately to blame for my weight gain, but the lack of any real financial constraint was making it all possible.

When I look back at pictures, I'm able to somewhat piece together my weight trajectory. At the end of grad school, I clocked in at 165 to 170 pounds. Over the next several years, as I entered the working world and married, I started to noticeably gain weight. By early 2011, when Anne Marie and I decided to move from Boston to DC, I weighed roughly 200 pounds, which made me solidly overweight. But it was in Washington where I *really* started to pack on the pounds.

I took a new job and, during my first two and a half years living in DC, managed to add 50 more pounds— that's nearly 10 additional pounds every six months! At the start of 2014, I was thirty-five years old and weighed a staggering 250 pounds. From a medical perspective, I was classified as "severely obese."

The weight was beginning to take its toll on my health. I'd started taking blood pressure medicine a few years earlier, but the doctor had to keep upping my dosage. At my annual physical, my doctor informed me that my cholesterol was also above normal and I was going to have to start taking medicine to manage that as well. She gave me six months to see if I could bring my cholesterol under control through a combination of exercise and healthier eating. My affluence was literally making me sick, and what the doctor said set off alarm bells in my mind. All the same, I was at a loss as to what to do about it. I'd been on diets before and always ended up right back where I started—ultimately, in fact, heavier than ever.

I was also looking pretty rough. My colleagues joked with me that I "had a face made for radio," which was unfortunate because my job required me to occasionally appear on TV. It was all in jest, but it was clearly a sign that I was getting too damn fat.

Of course, I realized that I was getting fatter and fatter, but I felt helpless to get a handle on it. In hindsight, it's obvious what was going on. Being new to DC, my wife and I wanted to sample all of the city's culinary delights, and so we continued the habit of eating out that we had developed back in Boston. Even when we didn't eat out, takeout was frequently the option of least resistance because we had a new infant at home. Plus, I had taken up a regular snacking habit.

So there I was at the start of 2014: 250 pounds and severely obese. And that's when I had the good fortune to sit down with my friend and coauthor Chris Payne. Our fateful conversation took place after I'd appeared in a video for Bloomberg discussing a recent event in the news. It started something like this:

Rob: Did you see my latest video?
Chris: Yeah, I saw it. Good job.
Rob: Thanks. But fuck, man! I'm getting fat.
Chris: One could say that. One could also say that you *are* fat.

Ouch! But I knew he was right. Over the next few minutes, Chris and I discussed my weight problem, and I found out that he, too, had once been obese but had somehow managed to get his weight under control. Chris helped me realize that there was no real mystery to how I'd gained so much weight: I simply ate too much, and the simple solution to my problem was to eat less. He pointed out that, despite all the talk about metabolism or genetics, the biggest difference between fat people and thin people is behavior. Thin people eat less than fat ones.

I pushed back, of course, because it was easier to make excuses than to accept responsibility for my situation. But this conversation helped us both realize that certain key behaviors affect weight, all of which can be explained by the same principles both of us had studied for years: the principles of economics.

HOW SOCIETY GOT FAT

Before we can understand how to change our behavior in order to lose weight, it's helpful to understand how we as a society got fat in the first place.

Theories abound as to what led to our current obesity epidemic. Recently, many scientists have started pointing to a lack of diversity in our gut bacteria (also known as our microbiome) as a likely culprit.[3] Others suggest that chemicals called phthalates, which are commonly found in plastic and a variety of household products, disrupt the body's hormonal system, thus causing weight gain.[4] Others theorize that too much weight gain by a mother during pregnancy can predispose the baby to being overweight—which then percolates throughout childhood and into adult life. Apparently, receiving too many antibiotics as a child can exert a similar effect. Meanwhile, certain genetic conditions play a role, which is one reason why obesity runs in families.[5]

We are not in a position to refute any of this important scientific work, but, on the whole, we think the problem is much more straightforward: we have gotten fat simply because we eat too much food. Why? Because most of us have access to much more food than we need. In economic terms, we could say that there is an oversupply, or glut, of food in many parts of the world. Increased supply with concomitant lower prices has pushed the boundaries of our self-control to the breaking point. Throughout this book, we call this condition "abundance."

Pretty much every commonly held explanation for obesity can be explained by abundance. One of the most widely read books on weight gain (and a favorite of ours), *Why We Get Fat: And What to Do About It* by Gary Taubes, dedicates pages and pages to convincing us that "we do not get fat because we overeat; we get fat because the carbohydrates in our diet make us fat."[6] Specifically, these types of nutrients trigger the hormone insulin, thereby signaling to your body the need to store fat; eating too many carbohydrates will therefore result in excess fat. For good reasons that we will explain later, we don't doubt that it's best to avoid eating too much pasta, rice, sugar, and bread, but our overconsumption of these carbohydrates, either turning up on our dinner plate or as a snack, has been caused by their abundance. By way of example, obesity rates are often higher in poorer sections of rich countries precisely because, thanks to mass production techniques, these sections of the population fill themselves up on carbohydrate-heavy foods, which, in the past few decades, have become extremely inexpensive to produce. These products can be sold cheaply and therefore are more appealing than their healthier counterparts; as a result, they are bought in large quantities.

Meanwhile, much has been written about how stress leads to overeating. As we told you earlier, one of the reasons that Chris ate so much when he worked in London was because he felt stressed out about his job. But the fact of the matter is, if he hadn't had access to so much food, no amount of stress could have made him gain weight. Likewise, a genetic predisposition to being overweight could go unnoticed for generations in the same family if food was relatively scarce.[7]

Data provided by the World Health Organization (WHO) provide clear evidence that income and abundance (caused by productivity gains that lead to higher incomes in the first place) are associated with obesity. It's difficult to look at the chart on page 22 without concluding that the richer a country is, the more likely it is to have an obesity problem.

Percentage of adults that are overweight by World Bank income group

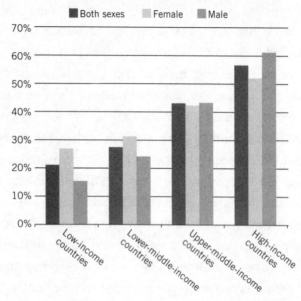

Source: World Health Organization. Being overweight is defined as having a body mass index score of 25 or more.

There are many reasons why we overeat, and certainly some foods are better for us than others. But as this chart shows, without access to the huge supply of food currently at our disposal, obesity rates would not be what they are today: poorer countries have a lower incidence of people being overweight than richer countries do.

The US Centers for Disease Control and Prevention (CDC) estimates that 36 percent of adult Americans are obese, while about 33 percent are overweight—so nearly 70 percent of the population is either overweight or obese.[8] It hasn't always been so. In 1970 only about 15 percent of the population would have been classified as obese and about 32 percent as overweight—for a combined total of 47 percent.[9] Okay, so Americans haven't been thin for a while, but they have grown much rounder in the last few decades.

And it's not just an American problem. The WHO estimates that 35 percent of the world's adults are overweight and 11 percent are obese.[10] The majority of the earth's population now lives in countries where obesity and weight-related diseases kill more people than starvation or undernourishment.[11]

By way of example, obesity is also an issue in France, which many Americans assume is populated entirely by waif-thin models. In 1997 only 37 percent of French citizens were overweight or obese, but by 2007, nearly 50 percent were classified as such.[12] This is shocking considering that same year, French-born author Mireille Guiliano published a bestselling book in America entitled *French Women Don't Get Fat*. Turns out, they do.

So why are we eating so much?

In 2003 three Harvard University economists, David Cutler, Ed Glaeser, and Jesse Shapiro, published an article in the *Journal of Economic Perspectives* entitled

"Why Have Americans Become More Obese?" In it they blamed mass production techniques related to processing and packing food—specifically atmospheric control, preventing spoilage due to microorganisms, flavor preservation, moisture preservation, and temperature control—which have advanced considerably since the early 1970s. These technological innovations have greatly reduced the amount of time it takes to prepare a meal while simultaneously giving us access to a wider variety of food. More food, more kinds of food, plus more time to eat the food: it all comes back to abundance.[13]

If you pause and think about your own habits, you can probably observe the central truth in this idea. When was the last time you cooked a meal completely from scratch at home? How often do you eat out? Does most of the food you're eating come in a plastic bag, a box, or a can? This doesn't necessarily mean you have to demonize all processed foods or fast-food restaurants, but because they generally contain many more calories than food prepared with basic ingredients at home, it's clear they play a central role in our ever-increasing waistlines.

More processed and mass-produced food explains a large part of the problem; after all, the whole point of a production line is to increase supply, lowering prices along the way. Indeed, the most important of all economics books, *The Wealth of Nations*, written back in 1776 by the Scottish political economist and moral philosopher Adam Smith, opens with an explanation of how the revolution in production techniques was enabling exponential increases in output. These techniques, combined with the advanced specialization of tasks among workers (what Smith called the division of labor), has enabled the gross domestic product (GDP) per capita in the United States to increase by roughly twenty-five times—2,500 percent—between when Adam Smith wrote and today.[14]

Our obesity epidemic suggests that the more food that has been produced, the more food we've eaten. If you still doubt whether there is a glut of food that is responsible for making us fat, just look at the table below, published by the US National Institutes of Health. In the twenty years between 1993 and 2013 alone, it is shocking to see how much average portion sizes have increased.

Comparison of Portions and Calories Between 1993 and 2013				
	1993		2013	
	Portion	Calories	Portion	Calories
Bagel	3 inches in diameter	140	6 inches in diameter	350
Cheeseburger	1	333	1	590
Spaghetti with meatballs	1 cup, 3 small meatballs	500	2 cups, 3 large meatballs	1,020
Soda	6.5 ounces	82	20 ounces	250
Blueberry muffin	1.5 ounces	210	5 ounces	500

Source: US National Institutes of Health[15]

Even so, the processed-food revolution tells only part of the story. Higher incomes have also played a role in changing our preferences and expectations of how much food we want to eat. Not only has supply increased dramatically, but also demand has shifted upward. This is because consumption is predominantly determined by income—a point that was central to the twentieth century's most famous economist, John Maynard Keynes, in the analysis of consumption in his landmark book *The General Theory of Employment, Interest and Money*, first published in 1936. "Men are disposed," Keynes wrote, "as a rule and on the average, to increase their consumption as their income increases."[16] And while the British economist wasn't referring specifically to eating, time has shown that this statement is as equally applicable to food as it is to anything else we buy. Earning more doesn't just mean we can afford more; it means that we actually prefer to spend and consume more. We want bigger houses, better cars, fancier gadgets, and more of pretty much everything, including food.

The charts below are sending a clear message. You don't have to be a statistician to see a well-defined relationship over the past forty years between increases in the daily consumption of calories, being overweight, and income.

INTRODUCTION

US income per capita and US calorie intake per capita

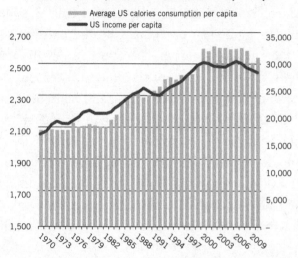

Average US calories consumption per capita
US income per capita

Incidence of being overweight and income per capita in the US

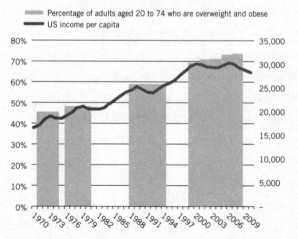

Percentage of adults aged 20 to 74 who are overweight and obese
US income per capita

Sources: US Census, National Center for Health Statistics[17]

On the surface, this doesn't make much sense. We'd be more inclined to think as Adam Smith did: "The desire of food is limited in every man by the narrow capacity of the human stomach," he wrote in *The Wealth of Nations*. "But the desire of the conveniences and ornaments of building, dress, equipage, and household furniture seems to have no limit or certain boundary."[18] Put simply, Smith assumed wrongly but entirely reasonably that no matter how much money we have and how much we spend, humans would always consume a certain quantity of food—enough to enable them to go on living.

So why should rising incomes influence how much we eat?

For the answer, we find it useful to turn to another economist, Tibor Scitovsky. Keynes had previously put forth the notion that consumption behavior could be influenced by a number of subjective factors, including enjoyment, shortsightedness, generosity, miscalculation, ostentation, and extravagance, rather than simply an objective factor like income. In his 1976 book *The Joyless Economy: An Inquiry into Human Satisfaction and Consumer Dissatisfaction* (sure to be your next book club selection!), Scitovsky took his analysis of the role of enjoyment one step further by splitting it into two distinct emotions: comfort and pleasure.

Comfort, as defined by Scitovsky, is the feeling we get when our level of arousal is just right. Meanwhile, both overstimulation and understimulation are uncomfortable states. Hunger, for instance, can be viewed as a form of understimulation—a disturbance that needs to be eliminated by eating, which returns us to an optimum level of arousal, and, thus, a general feeling of comfort.[19]

Using Scitovsky's own terminology, feelings of comfort come when we get to a certain "speed" of arousal. Pleasure, on the other hand, is a bit like acceleration and deceleration. We feel pleasure as we move from a state of overstimulation or understimulation to a state of optimum stimulation (comfort). When we eat, we feel pleasure by "speeding up and away" from the disturbance that hunger causes.

But problems arise because the pleasure that we experience by getting our stimulation just right is not necessarily eliminated once we arrive at that optimal level. Many drivers feel comfortable when cruising at fifty-five miles per hour but will accelerate above this speed because of the pleasure generated simply by accelerating.

In other words, while we feel comfortable at an optimum state, we feel pleasure when experiencing further stimulating activity, even if that stimulation leads us to a place where we don't want to be. We eat to appease our hunger, and therefore we must be hungry to really enjoy eating. But once we start eating, the pleasure of doing so doesn't stop just because we have satiated our appetites. We often continue to stimulate ourselves by eating to the point of feeling uncomfortable.

You can see this idea at work in the stories we told you about how each of us got fat. Chris was understimulated at work, so he turned to food to provide short-term arousal. And even after he'd eaten enough to feel satiated, he continued to pig out and snack in order to maintain that sense of stimulation. Likewise with Rob: a key part of finding new stimuli from his surroundings in Boston and Washington, DC, involved eating out.

By this point, you might have recognized an uncomfortable truth in our explanation for why so many of us are overweight. In a world where millions suffer from real starvation and malnutrition, some of us have attained a level of wealth and accompanying boredom that we literally try to eat our way out of. Our narratives are a perfect example of overeating caused by not only an increase in the supply of cheap food at low prices but also a desire to eat a greater variety of tastier, more enticing, and fattening meals and snacks. It is a problem of both supply and demand.

Still, it's not for us to say whether you recognize yourself in our narratives of getting fat. The reasons *we* overate may not be the same reasons *you* overeat. But ultimately, we have learned that the only solution is to eat less. And, for the rest of this book, we're going to show you how to do just that.

HOW TWO ECONOMISTS APPROACH
THE PROBLEM OF WEIGHT LOSS

You've read our personal stories of weight gain, and you've read our explanation of why so many people overeat. Now, what can you do about it?

INTRODUCTION

Each of the following chapters provides specific and straightforward tips on how to train yourself to eat less in a world where food is abundant. As we explained earlier, although this advice is designed to be practical and not theoretical, it is based on key economic principles that explain why this approach works.

In chapter 1, "Scarcity (Why You Need to Weigh Yourself Every Day)," we explain that a diet is what we call a "self-imposed eating-austerity program." Just as a country might impose spending cuts today in order to avoid an economic crisis tomorrow, a dieter must learn how to reduce the amount of food he or she eats today in order to avoid a future health crisis. One reason this is so difficult is because eating less means you are going to, at times, experience hunger—a state that is uncomfortable but necessary if you want to lose weight. We offer a variety of ways to mentally battle the temptations to snack and overeat that are ever present, especially when you're feeling hungry. In particular, we explain, using behavioral economics, why weighing yourself every day will bolster your ability to make better decisions.

We, Rob and Chris, became fat because, in our daily lives, we encountered a glut of food but were essentially unconstrained by our budgets, creating a situation in which unbounded demand met practically unlimited supply. As chapter 2, "Abundance (Busting the Myth of Three Square Meals a Day)," discusses, this manifests partly through the expectation, prevalent in our society, that we should eat three square, or full-sized, meals a day. In outlining the economic history of this practice, we show that, in today's world, while eating three times a day is a good routine to stick to (especially if it helps you avoid snacking), only one of these meals should be square.

Good decision making requires good information, and good information means good data. In chapter 3, "Data (Be Calorie Conscious, Not a Calorie Counter)," we explain that there is an information gap between what you eat and the effect it has on your body. Fortunately, calorie data, provided by many restaurants and on packaged foods, can provide an effective signal, motivating you to make healthier decisions. Using this logic, we'll make an argument for being *calorie conscious* as opposed to being a *calorie counter*, which we believe turns data into an impossible-to-tame tyrant instead of an ally in your fight to keep weight off over the long term. In addition to calorie data, we'll show how experimenting with your body using a scale can help you determine what kind and quantity of food is right for you. The chapter ends with a plan for setting a long-term weight target that is achievable and realistic.

Dieters face many headwinds in their battle to lose weight and keep it off, not least of which is the food industry's constant efforts to encourage us to eat more. Chapter 4, "Buyer Beware (Don't Waste Time or Money on the Diet Industrial Complex)," employs concepts developed in behavioral economics to explain why we're so often influenced by misleading marketing and how to guard ourselves against these tactics. We explain the economic philosophy behind "buyer beware" and why, in a free-market economy, it's up to consumers to differentiate between genuinely valuable products/services and gimmicks designed to make us spend money on things we don't need.

In chapter 5, "Equilibrium (Variety May Be the Spice of Life, but It's Also Making You Fat)," we use consumer theory and the related law of diminishing returns to explain why, for many of us, the constant search for new eating experiences and variety is problematic for our waistlines. Following from this, we explain that a repetitive diet is a slimming diet and that if you want to maintain a healthy weight, you should limit the number and types of foods you eat. To illustrate this, we provide details on what we eat at home as well as some recommendations to help get you started. Using the same concept of equilibrium, we'll advise you on coming to terms with one of the harsher realities of weight loss: that dieting is a lifestyle that demands changing your eating habits for the long term. That said, the more you practice it, the easier it becomes.

At this point, it's important to stress that while we believe you should follow our advice closely, the Economists' Diet is specifically designed so that you can, at times, enjoy the basic pleasure that comes with eating your favorite foods. Any diet that prohibits the occasional splurge is doomed to failure because even the most motivated dieter has limits on how much he or she can sacrifice. In chapter 6, "Budgeting (How to Splurge and Still Lose Weight)," we employ the prisoner's dilemma, a favorite model of economists, to explain that feasting is a necessary part of human activity, and one that we need to embrace. While in current times we splurge more than ever, humans have always enjoyed overeating on certain occasions. The key to squaring this particular circle—and thus preventing the urge to splurge from making you fat—is to practice mini-feasting/mini-fasting, either by saving up calories in advance of a big meal or by paying off calorie debts after the occasion. Given the imperative to mini-feast/mini-fast, it becomes paramount not to waste calories on food you don't really enjoy.

We hope that in reading this book, you will learn some principles of economics and take inspiration from our personal stories. Most important, we hope we will convince you to give our behavioral approach to weight loss a try. We know from personal experience that eating less and avoiding temptation take practice and effort. Likewise, our behavioral recommendations will take time to put into action and perfect. But what makes them powerful is their simplicity and brevity. Taken together, our behavioral best practices provide an original approach to dieting, which, as we know from firsthand experience, enables dieters to achieve lasting weight loss. And trust us: if we can do it, so can you.

CHAPTER 1

SCARCITY

(Why You Need to Weigh Yourself Every Day)

Much like a serial gambler must learn to control his or her impulses in a world where lottery tickets and other games of chance can be purchased from the corner convenience store, someone who is trying to lose weight must train him or herself to eat less in a world where food is abundant. And short of exiling yourself to a desert island where your diet is limited to coconuts, native grasses, and fish you can catch with a spear you fashioned from a tree branch, you will find this easier said than done.

That's why we believe the only way to keep yourself honest when dieting is to weigh yourself each and every day. This is our first and perhaps most important piece of advice in the Economists' Diet, because it is an essential step toward behaving as if food is scarcer than it actually is. Scales don't lie, and by seeing that number in front of you—whether it's gone up or down since yesterday—you will be more likely to stay motivated in the face of inevitable temptation.

DIETING IS A SELF-IMPOSED
AUSTERITY EATING PLAN

As we told you in the introduction, Chris's tale of over-eating came to a dramatic end on a cold winter's morning in January 2004, when he stepped on the scale and discovered that he weighed a whopping 220 pounds. He was absolutely mortified by what he saw, but he knew he had nobody to blame but himself. Overweight for many years, Chris realized that this new high (or low, depending on how you look at it) was the direct result of his gluttony.

Like anyone who has experienced a similar moment of private despair over the state of his or her body, Chris desperately wanted to do something about it. But what? How was he going to break himself of the habits he'd been indulging in for much of his adult life? How was he going to avoid temptation when delicious food was readily available to him 24/7?

Chris decided to look at the problem through the lens of his profession. History has shown us that economic activity runs through regular periods of growth (booms) followed by regular periods of contraction (busts). In biblical times, we called this "seven years of abundance followed by seven years of famine." In the twentieth century, economists came to refer to this pattern as "the economic cycle."

Chris realized he'd been on a speculative boom with his body, taking full advantage of the abundance of food around him with little regard for the long-term consequences. He also knew that, as with the economy, a bust was inevitable: at some point, his recklessness was going to catch up with him, and he would be forced to cut back whether he wanted to or not. It was a depressing thought, but he knew he had to reverse the cycle.

To put it simply, Chris needed to put himself on a self-imposed austerity eating plan. In economics, when a government or institution enacts an austerity plan, it means cutting back radically on spending in order to save money. If government officials are smart, they start practicing austerity before it's necessary to ensure that the economy slows gently rather than crashes against a wall. Unfortunately, because austerity is so difficult and often makes people unhappy due to the sacrifices they're forced to make, it usually happens only after the bottom has fallen out. This is exactly what Greece experienced after 2009 when foreign banks and other lenders started demanding that the country pay back the money it had borrowed over the years. Greece had been on a credit-fueled spending spree, and when the party finally ended, its government was left with no easy way to clean up the mess. It wasn't a pretty picture, and, as we write this, the Greeks are still trying to dig themselves out of bankruptcy.

Chris didn't want to be like the Greeks. He didn't want to wait until it was too late—until his "creditors" (that is, his health) started calling in his debts. He was seeing the warning signs already. So he decided to impose eating austerity on himself, pretending that food was scarce, even though it wasn't.

It wasn't going to be fun. Austerity is never fun. And by definition, Chris was anything but austere. This, after all, is the guy who counts among his greatest creations the so-called Christmas lunch: a pre–December 25th celebration he shares with his pals that involves eating giant steaks, drinking copious amounts of red wine and beer, and rounding off the day with a large curry. Austere people are severe and stern (they aren't invited to Chris's Christmas lunch), and if they throw a party (which they probably won't), it's sure to be boring, and the food is likely to be cheap and insubstantial.

This is precisely why dieting is so hard. Because cutting back—especially when you feel like you don't have to—is not fun. But Chris knew that it's always smarter and less painful in the long run to self-impose austerity before you actually have to. (Just ask anyone trying to dig himself out of credit card debt.)

Why do we get caught up in these cycles of boom and bust, feast and famine? If we know the pattern, why do we keep repeating it? Simple: because humans naturally place too much value on present enjoyment over future enjoyment. We see this everywhere. On a macroeconomic level, we see it when governments throw too much money at entitlement programs or other expensive projects without calculating the costs to future generations who will inevitably have to pay for them. In our personal lives, it's often more enjoyable to spend money on a fancy dinner out tonight than to consider, for example, the full extent of the satisfaction that will come once a large enough deposit has been saved up to buy a house; or the pleasure from having saved prudently for retirement and having sufficient income to continue to enjoy vacations and spoil grandchildren.

This is true even for people who should know better. Chris once asked a Wall Street friend about his plans to save for the future and was amazed when his friend said he didn't need to save for retirement because he didn't expect to live that long. If his seventy-year-old self wasn't going to need the cash, why not blow it all now on a driving expedition through South America? Live for today, tomorrow be damned!

Talk about undervaluing the future! Certainly plenty of families have trouble making ends meet, let alone socking away money for later. But this was a guy who *worked with money for a living* and made more than a sufficient salary. Not only that, he was willfully ignoring the ample evidence showing that he is likely to live well into his seventies or eighties. One only hopes he wises up sooner rather than later.

We may be shocked at Wall Street Guy's flippant attitude toward saving for retirement, but if you've ever struggled with your weight, you've likely made the exact same miscalculation. By persistently overeating, we set aside concern for our future selves, despite knowing full well that our choices today will adversely affect our health and happiness tomorrow.

As rational as we, Rob and Chris, are about financial savings, we have succumbed to shortsightedness and miscalculation when it comes to our eating habits. In fact, when Chris was in his early twenties and used to talk with people about his weight problem, he leaned on the same measly excuse about how he'd probably die early in order to avoid facing the reality of his overeating. And he's heard the same justification from the mouths of other overweight and obese friends. (Of course, if he *had* continued to overeat, Chris might have eventually proved himself right.)

Just like a thrifty individual saving prudently for retirement, or a government curbing spending now in order to be able to afford entitlement programs in the future, a dieter needs to eat less now in order to enhance the enjoyment, quality, and, most likely, length of his or her life down the line. By making a commitment to lose weight, you are essentially recognizing that the satisfaction (delayed gratification) of being thin and healthy tomorrow will be greater than any satisfaction (instant gratification) you get from indulging in that extra slice of pizza or cake today. We won't say that thinking in these terms will make dieting easier, but it will help you stay focused and motivated knowing that you are working toward a long-term goal.

This motivation is necessary because limiting our intake of food is harder than it has ever been before. For much of human history, we were thin because food was relatively hard to come by, and we engaged in more rigorous daily activities. As a result, our instincts told us it was wise to eat whatever potables we could get our hands on.

But new mass production techniques have given rise to our current age of abundance with, more often than not, too much rather than too little food. With our instincts still telling us to eat what's in front of us, it's no wonder that nearly 70 percent of Americans are overweight.

It's All About Delaying Gratification

Before dieting, both of us were far too likely to succumb to the pleasure of instant gratification: for instance, reaching for a Snickers bar at four in the afternoon because we were hungry between meals.

In this instance, learning about delayed gratification involved avoiding a sugar rush followed by a crash and, instead, waiting a couple of hours to enjoy a sensible meal.

Eating less is difficult not only because it curtails instant gratification and goes against our innate inclination to stuff our faces but also because it gives rise to hunger. The sensation of hunger is a natural, necessary biological phenomenon that signals when we need nourishment. Unfortunately, when we become used to overeating, this signal goes a little wackadoodle and tells us to eat when we really don't need food. For example, a 2016 study of contestants on the reality show *The Biggest Loser*, in which contestants compete to see who can lose the most weight, found that their levels of the hormone leptin plummeted after extreme weight loss.[1] Leptin, produced by fat cells, helps control feelings of hunger by signaling the brain that the body has sufficient stores of fat. Scientists believe that a drop in a person's leptin level induces a more acute sense of hunger, leaving those who struggle with overeating feeling hungrier than they would otherwise. Nature is nothing if not ironic.

Humans hate being hungry, and why shouldn't we? Hunger is supposed to be uncomfortable because it's designed to motivate us to ingest calories in order to produce the energy we need to survive. But when our body starts to crave too much food, we need to outsmart it by choosing not to eat. This is why dieting is so hard: because we have to pretend food is scarce when it's obviously not.

The temptation to break your diet will be intense, even painful, at times. It will be difficult to stay the course, but if you think like an economist and trust that you are adopting austerity for the benefit of your future self, you can succeed. The rest of this chapter will show you how.

OVERCOMING THE FEAR OF HUNGER

It may sound like a tough message, but losing weight and keeping it off require a fundamental alteration in your attitude and behavior. More than anything else, eating austerity requires that you get used to being hungry sometimes and avoid the urge to satisfy this feeling by reaching for a candy bar, a bag of chips, or the multitude of other snacks available in the aisles of your grocery store. We know from personal experience that it gets much easier to cope with hunger pangs as the diet progresses, but knowing that won't make the first few months any easier.

Frankly, we know that this message will frighten many people. The fear of hunger is probably the biggest problem we've faced when introducing others to our dieting ideas. But we've come to understand that, diet or no diet, you should probably feel hungry just as often as—if not more than—you feel completely full. After all, hunger is nothing more than the body's way of alerting the brain that it is time to eat again. Therefore, a dieter needs to come off eating autopilot and learn how to listen to his or her body.

We are not claiming that this is easy to do. Unfortunately, the supply of food has increased much more quickly than human biology has evolved to adapt to it, which means we are likely, at least in part, still driven by hunter-gatherer thinking and physiology. After all, even though modern humans have inhabited the world for more than 300,000 years, sedentary agricultural societies have existed only for about 10,000 years. (The Western European economy was not transformed fully to one of plant and animal domestication until 5,500 years ago.) As we'll explain in chapter 4, this doesn't mean we recommend following the Paleo diet, which stresses the need to eat more of the kinds of foods that were eaten by humans before the adoption of agriculture; it just means that we know we are likely preprogrammed to eat all that is in front of us. As explained in Marshall Sahlins's classic anthropological text *Stone Age Economics*, which described the ways in which our hunter-gatherer predecessors procured and ate food, this make-hay-while-the-sun-shines attitude made perfect sense in a world where people were listening to signals from their bodies before heading out on the next hunting expedition. It's obviously less helpful when food is abundant and requires little effort to obtain.

The hard truth about the Economists' Diet, and all diets that actually work, is that you are going to feel hungry at times. And while we can talk theory all day long, we know that the hunger experienced while on a diet is deeply personal. Coming to terms with hunger, and adjusting how you respond to it, will probably be one of the most important things you do in your quest to lose weight. If you're overweight or obese today, you're likely accustomed to satiating your desire to eat nearly any time hunger rears its head. Both of us can relate, but this behavior has to stop.

Prior to losing weight, both of us would quickly find something to eat whenever we felt even just a twinge of hunger. This doesn't necessarily mean we ran to a restaurant and scarfed down a gut-busting meal at the first rumblings in our tummies, but through snacking or other means, we always kept hunger at bay. And as we've already discussed, there weren't any real financial or economic constraints stopping us from doing so. As far as hunger was concerned, we could have near-instant gratification.

SCARCITY

Losing weight would be a lot easier if we could simply flip a switch to turn off hunger. Notwithstanding the claims of some "miracle" pills currently being marketed—of which we are very dubious—such a technology simply does not exist from our point of view. And while some quick-fix diets claim to overcome hunger, such diets are, as we explain later in the book, completely unsustainable. In truth, hunger simply has to be dealt with. But how?

To start, we need to emphasize that hunger is very different from starvation. In our culture, people often say "I'm starving," "I'm famished," or "I'm so hungry I could die" to describe normal, healthy feelings of hunger. Such words should probably be wiped from our collective lexicon. Starvation is a real phenomenon that affects far too many in this world, but we're confident that anyone picking up this book has probably never experienced true starvation—that is, extreme, prolonged hunger; not what you experience after going a few hours between meals. You're not starving, you're hungry, and that's an okay thing to be.

Thinking back, when was the last time you let yourself go hungry for any sustained period? We'd wager that in a world where food is so cheap and convenient, sustained hunger will be a new experience for most of our readers; it certainly was for us when we started down the path of weight loss.

It's important to recognize that hunger won't kill you, though it may jolt your body and consciousness. The experience of hunger is subjective, but we can all relate to the basic idea: it's a twinge in your stomach that says "Feed me now." In our case, interpreting hunger differently was mostly a test of will—specifically, willing ourselves to take a step back and examine the sensation before acting instinctively to satiate our desire to eat.

Try This Now

Feeling hungry, but it's not time to eat? We've asked dieters and nondieters alike what their number one tip is for avoiding snacking and ignoring hunger. Across the board, the answer was: drink something instead. Some suggested plain old water, others recommended peppermint tea or coffee (plain black or with just a dash of milk). Distracting yourself was another top tip, since we often feel hunger when we're bored. Go for a walk, strike up a conversation, do some urgent task. Properly distracted, you'll likely forget that you were ever hungry in the first place.

One of the questions we've learned to ask ourselves is whether what we are feeling is *real* hunger. For instance, are we "really" hungry because it's one o'clock, and we haven't touched anything since breakfast at seven that morning? Or do we merely feel a stitch of hunger because it's been two hours since breakfast, and our body is digesting our last meal?

It's amazing how the body works. Surely we've all experienced the following: stuffing yourself at a special occasion only to wake up the following morning feeling ravenously hungry. But are you *really* hungry? As the two of us addressed the fear of hunger over the years and learned to ignore these kinds of hunger pangs, we realized that they tend to disappear after a few minutes. Early in his diet, Chris used the notion of "fake" hunger as a way to avoid snacking temptation. How was it possible, he asked himself, to have eaten breakfast, plus three full meals the day before, and yet still feel hungry at ten in the morning? Surely these were the same false signals that had led him to obesity in the first place. And soon enough, he discovered an amazing thing: unlike real hunger, these short-term hunger pangs often passed within a few minutes.

Strategy Number One for Overcoming the Fear of Hunger
Wait it out.

We highly recommend always asking yourself whether you're experiencing real hunger, given what you may have eaten the night before or earlier in the day. At the very least, don't immediately satiate the hunger. Harness your willpower to give your body a few minutes to adjust; that rumbling in your stomach may dissipate without you needing to snack. Of course, if the pangs don't go away after a few minutes, then it's probably fair to conclude that you need to eat. But before you grab that cookie or some other filling but unhealthy snack, take a moment to focus on what your body *needs*. If it's an hour before lunch, can you wait it out? You probably can, but if you can't, try eating the bare minimum of what you need to stave off the hunger. A piece of fruit or a handful of almonds might not be as tempting as that cookie, but they will satisfy you long enough that you can make it to your next meal without adding too much to your calorie count that day.

Willpower isn't everything, of course. Surrounding yourself with like-minded people can also prove helpful. For example, Rob had the benefit of Chris's company when he began his weight loss journey at the beginning of 2014. By the time Rob decided to lose weight, Chris had a decade of experience dealing with hunger and weight management, so when Rob complained about how hungry he was, Chris could prod Rob in the right direction: "You can do this. Is it really that bad?" "I promise it will get better with time." "I've been there; keep going." "Keep your eyes on the prize." Don't diet alone unless you absolutely have to. The buddy system works.

Having a receptive spouse or roommate may also boost your chances of success. Rob's wife, who has always kept her weight under control, led a lifestyle that naturally supported Rob's new austerity-driven food regimen. On evenings when Rob felt hungry, Anne Marie wasn't sitting across the table eating pizza or snacking on a bowl of chips. If they both ate a big lunch, they'd have a small dinner or skip it altogether. Having a like-minded person nearby not only helped reduce temptation but also provided Rob with an environment that set him up to succeed.

Try This Now

Next time you are chatting with your spouse, boyfriend, girlfriend, or any friend you feel comfortable confiding in, start a conversation about your weight and your plans for weight loss. Having them on your side will be hugely helpful—and force you to be accountable, knowing they will likely be watching for signs of progress.

Perhaps the best advice either one of us received about managing hunger came from an ex–currency trader whom Chris spoke to about weight control. Now, if you saw this guy, you would find it hard to believe that he ever needed help controlling his weight. He was thin by anyone's standards, but he told Chris that he worked hard to keep himself that way. How? To use his words, he said he often "enjoyed feeling hungry," a notion that would probably confuse many people. But to him it signaled that he was succeeding in controlling his weight. Having come to understand that hunger was sometimes necessary, he'd accepted it and even embraced it.

Things we did to distract ourselves from hunger in the first few weeks of our diets:
- got back (after a fifteen-year break) to practicing the piano;

- unexpectedly developed an interest in cleaning and organizing our homes;
- cleared our homes of snacks and sugary treats;
- told all our friends and family that we were on a diet;
- went for some long walks, putting as much distance as possible between ourselves and our kitchens; and
- continued to drink beer (some sacrifices are too much to ask) but made sure our social gatherings didn't also involve excessive eating.

Neither of us particularly *enjoys* being hungry. In fact, if you ask our wives, they'll tell you that we're often grumpy and ill-tempered when real hunger strikes. Being "hangry"—anger caused by hunger—is a natural emotion for many people, including us. Even so, it was important for both of us early on in our diets to learn to associate hunger with being on the right track. To this day, Rob sometimes imagines himself pumping his fist in the air when he's hungry. He's putting his "hanger" to use, feeling like he's raging against a machine whose sole purpose is to entice him to eat too much. Ultimately, though, real hunger indicates that a mini-fast after a splurge has lasted long enough to be successful, and while knowing that may not make us happy, it certainly does put our minds at ease.

Fear of hunger is probably why so many people fail at dieting. We know this not only because we've heard it so many times but also because it's evident in most fad diets. Many of these diets employ the economic concept of substitution: that is, eating the so-called diet version of a favorite food instead of simply eating less of it; or cutting out a specific type of food only to eat more of everything else. And then there are the even more sinister diet plans that involve "miracle" pills and supplements that don't seem to require any change in your eating habits at all. These diets and fads play on the dieter's fear of hunger, and inevitably they fail because the only sustainable solution to overeating is to eat less, which will inevitably involve hunger. Of course, food companies can't make money by telling you to *not* consume something, so it's no wonder these fads and marketing tricks persist.

So, for now, here's a quick pep talk: embrace hunger with open arms. We know from our own experience that losing weight without ever feeling hungry is impossible. Accepting this truth is critical to preparing yourself for successful, long-lasting weight loss. There is simply no way to avoid hunger if you want to lose weight, so you might as well get used to the idea now rather than later. But here's the good news: hunger won't kill you, and over time, you'll start to experience it differently.

We were both hungry and unhappy during the first few weeks of our diets. But as we grew accustomed to eating less, the intensity of our hunger abated. We got used to feeling hungry and it became a normal part of our daily routines. Now that we've lost the weight, we experience hunger less but still use it as a valuable signal as we continue to manage our weight.

We embraced hunger, and you can, too. The first step is acknowledging that it must be done.

DON'T DESPAIR: HELP IS AT HAND— FROM ECONOMICS!

Given what you have read so far, we hope you have a better understanding of why you are overweight. But you're probably still waiting for that universal magic bullet, the one secret to stopping in its tracks the temptation to overeat.

Okay. We're going to tell you, but you're probably not going to like it.

Your biggest ally in the battle to lose weight is weighing yourself every day. Stepping on that dreaded scale each morning and staring at that number looking back at you will be your sucker punch to hunger; it has been for us and several of our friends. Let us explain.

These days, the field of economics is dominated largely by micro-economists: those who focus on small-scale interactions, transactions, and outcomes. They spend a lot of time trying to evaluate the monetary incentives that motivate people to opt for one choice over another. The idea for taxing cigarettes, for instance, wasn't plucked out of thin air. Economists have to set an appropriate levy that is not overly punitive, raises meaningful amounts of money for government, and incentivizes people to smoke less. Likewise, economists calibrate subsidies for green energy or on agricultural products in order to produce a particular outcome.

Incentives often work in complicated and unexpected ways. But sometimes they can be quite straightforward. Ask an economist how to accomplish something, and he or she will probably ask you how much, monetarily speaking, it is worth to you. This thought experiment basically pits your expected future hunger against an amount of money that will enable you to overcome hunger or any other temptation to give up on your diet. We've all played this game in some form or other, generally when we ask our friends, "Would you do x for a million dollars?"

According to this way of thinking, one could diet successfully if offered enough of a monetary incentive to do so. For example, two friends might start a diet and pledge to pay each other a prearranged sum if one of them fails to lose an agreed-upon number of pounds within a specific time. If both meet the target, no money changes hands.

Rob actually tried something like this with his friend Jonathan. In March 2009, well before Rob had reached his highest weight, he and Jonathan entered into an agreement with the goal of shedding a few pounds. Both of them had gained weight since college and were rapidly approaching 200 pounds. According to the terms of their agreement, they would have to pay $500 and surrender their passport to the other person if they didn't get their weight below 175 pounds by Thanksgiving. The friend would keep the surrendered passport until the other reached the 175-pound target. For two guys who like to travel, this should have been ample incentive. Unfortunately, neither Rob nor Jonathan met the goal because neither was willing to enforce the contract, and they both knew it; in fact, neither lost any weight at all! Of course, if you want to enter into that kind of bargain with a fellow dieter, then you certainly have our blessings; we are economists, after all. We just don't think this is a workable solution for many people.

Our argument against using monetary bribes to trick yourself into dieting does not mean that we discount the use of financial incentives, such as taxes on sugary drinks or the promise of cheaper insurance when trying to lose weight. It's just that we prefer to look for guidance in a newer burgeoning area of economics: behavioral economics.

OVERCOMING THE TEMPTATION TO OVEREAT, ESPECIALLY WHEN HUNGER HITS

Work by two behavioral economists, Sendhil Mullainathan and Eldar Shafir, on the subject of scarcity provides the perfect complement to our argument. The concept of scarcity serves as the foundation for mainstream economics because the fact that we don't have unlimited resources forces us to make choices about what we buy. Indeed, Professor Lionel Robbins of the London School of Economics famously defined economics back in the 1930s as "the science which studies human behavior as a relationship between ends and scarce means which have alternative uses." But as Mullainathan and Shafir point out, scarcity—particularly the experience of severe scarcity—often leads to bad or irrational decision making.

Mullainathan and Shafir apply their ideas primarily to the practice of payday lending, a business that enables people to take out small, short-term loans at very high interest rates when they are hard up for cash. Payday lending can make sense under certain circumstances: for example, it could be cheaper to pay your electricity bill with a $100 one-month loan at a 20 percent interest rate—paying back the lender $120 one month later—than to pay the reconnection costs that come from being cut off for nonpayment. Yet all too often, borrowers don't repay the loan quickly enough, and the interest and fees compound over time. Note: a 20 percent monthly interest rate equates to a 792 percent annual interest rate! In our example, if the borrower ends up paying back that $100 plus interest one year later (rather than one month later), he or she will have to fork over a staggering $892 to the lender.

The question is, why do payday borrowers so often find themselves trapped in an ever-increasing cesspit of debt, forever rolling over their loans, when it makes so much more sense to pay off these debts the moment an opportunity arises? Mullainathan and Shafir posit that the experience of scarcity (being short of cash) is so overwhelming that those in this situation often fail to think clearly and therefore act less rationally than they should. The borrower is so preoccupied over dealing with the upcoming bill or expense that he or she is utterly incapable of seeing the big picture. "Scarcity," they write, "leads us to borrow and pushes us deeper into scarcity."[2]

So what's all this got to with dieting? Well, as we have said, going on a diet is a form of scarcity, the only difference being that it is self-imposed. The resulting hunger often leads the dieter into a mental tunnel in which the only thing he or she can think about is food. When dieters experience moments of hunger and temptation, it is not just hunger that makes them want to break the diet; it is the fact that the experience of lacking food negatively impacts clear thinking.

If you have ever failed at dieting, you probably know exactly what we are talking about. It used to be the same story for us, and we know it's the same story for many people we've talked to. You started out the diet as a rational human being who knew what he had to do to lose weight—and why it was important to do so. But within a few hours, you started thinking about nothing except food, consumed (no pun intended) by the desire to satiate your hunger. And because you were so focused on feeling hungry, you started to forget why you set out on the diet in the first place. You knew you had to eat less, you knew you were going to be hungry, and you also knew you weren't going to starve by eating less. But in a moment of weakness, you couldn't think straight. You grabbed that chocolate bar or bag of chips and ate it anyway. The hunger pangs soon abated, and you immediately castigated yourself for your lack of willpower; you could hardly understand why you broke the diet you were so committed to just a few hours ago.

Because hunger creates such tunnel vision, a dieter needs constant and permanent vigilance. Indeed, we know from personal experience that the self-imposed austerity eater needs to be able to lean on a powerful device to overcome those moments of temptation. And we know from experience that the daily weigh-in is *the* one device that has successfully thrust vigilance upon us, especially when hunger pushes the "bandwidth tax on thinking"[3] to the max. It is both the carrot and the stick. If you wake up in the morning and see that you have lost a pound since yesterday, the joy you feel can keep you going for the whole day, fully inoculated against temptation. Alternatively, if your weigh-in tells you that yesterday's splurge has undone two days of good dieting work, you become newly resolved to skip the blueberry muffin on your morning coffee run.

The scale hasn't budged for four days! What do I do?

- Keep up with your daily weigh-in.
- Consider eating less. It may be time to reduce the number of calories you eat each day.
- Now might be the time to make a food diary. Are you fully aware and/or being totally honest with yourself about what you're eating?

- Eat fewer carbohydrates (bread, pasta, rice, sugar).
- Every time you feel the need to snack, drink something instead; say, a tea or coffee (definitely no sugar).
- Don't eat out again until you've dropped more weight.
- Make sure your daytime activity level hasn't dropped.
- Are you getting enough sleep? Tiredness can lead to increased snacking.
- Drink more water; a change in diet may have made you constipated.
- Change your scale; perhaps it's old and not to be trusted.
- *Keep the faith!* Trust us: if you keep at it, your weight will soon start to fall.

Even if you don't like what you're seeing on the scale, you need to stick to this essential habit. Forming healthy habits requires persistent practice and taking no breaks from the routine.

Of course, we know there will be some random variability along the way or that sometimes the scale will seem to get stuck at a certain weight no matter what you do. Maybe you'll feast at your favorite restaurant and weigh less the next morning. Maybe you'll have a very disciplined day of eating—say, yogurt for breakfast, a salad for lunch, and an apple for dinner—and weigh more the next morning. When that kind of thing happens, you might be tempted to throw in the towel and throw your scale out the window. Likewise, disillusionment is likely to set in when your weight plateaus for a few days. Weight loss goes in spits and spurts. We would lose a few pounds, and then our weight would stabilize, even while we worked hard to keep our calorie intake low. But if we kept at the diet, we started losing weight again a few days or perhaps a week later. Dieting can seem tough when you hit one of these weight plateaus, but the only response is to persevere.

Despite these occasional anomalies on the scale, what has really surprised us is the remarkable consistency we can see between what we eat one day and what we weigh the next. We have much more to say about this in chapter 3.

Some may argue that obsessing over your daily weight is not healthy. By constantly monitoring your weight, aren't you just replacing one unhealthy set of compulsions with another? We would disagree for many reasons. In order to stay on track, you need to measure your progress so you know what you're doing right and what you're doing wrong. And for that, there is simply no substitute for getting on the scale each day. But perhaps more important, your daily weigh-in provides the perfect counterbalance to the weak willpower and the tunnel-like focus on food that occurs when you are hungry.

Indeed, if you are overweight or obese and are unhappy about it, then it's safe to say that you did not get there through rational choice. So why shy away from adopting a habit that's going to help you solve your weight problem? Surely it is better to practice a daily ritual of stepping on the scale than to continue packing on the pounds.

And to those hiding from the scale, we say this: knowing your weight doesn't make you any more overweight than not knowing it. The same goes for other people knowing it. Before his conversation with Chris in early 2014, Rob had received feedback about his weight from only one person: his friend Arup. Upon seeing him for the first time in a few years, Arup, whom Rob had met in grad school, blurted out, "Rob, you've gotten fat!" Rob didn't hold the comment against Arup; after all, he was telling the truth, even if everyone else had remained tactfully silent on the matter.

The point of this story is that your friends and loved ones know you're overweight even if they don't say so. You're not hiding anything from anyone, so why not be equipped with a precise number that can help you manage the problem? If it's the first time you've stepped on a scale in a while, your weight may come as an unpleasant surprise. But after you get over the initial shock, you'll find that weighing yourself daily will provide you with the most powerful tool in your battle to lose weight.

A number of scientific studies provide evidence that weighing yourself daily helps with dieting, as we discuss in detail later in this chapter. But we would go even further. Indeed, we don't believe it's a coincidence that, in our experience, the thin people we know have generally been far more aware of their weight than friends and family who are overweight (and not dieting). This is illustrated perfectly by the following situation that took place a few months into 2014 after Rob had started dieting.

Rob and his family spent a week in Florida visiting his wife's sister, Mary, and brother-in-law David, both of whom are thin. Since Rob was still new to the principles of the Economists' Diet, he brought along his scale so he could continue his daily weigh-in. At some point, his brother-in-law stepped on the scale that Rob had left lying on their guest room floor.

David knew immediately that something was wrong. "Hey, Rob! Something's wrong with your scale. Mary! Come check this out!"

Mary came over and stepped on the scale. "Oh yes; this isn't right," she said.

Rob was confused. "What are you guys talking about?"

"There's just no way I'm this light," Mary said. "It's off by at least five pounds."

David added, "As much as I'd love for this to be my weight, I'm with Mary; this scale is definitely underreporting your weight by at least five or maybe six pounds."

After returning from vacation, Rob tested several other scales: David and Mary were right! They were so attuned to their own weight that they could easily identify a miscalibrated scale. Rob's scale was off by almost exactly six pounds—so rather than weighing about 204 pounds at the time, he was actually closer to 210 pounds. Rob felt a little bit of anguish upon discovering that he was heavier than he'd previously thought, but he accepted the facts and bought a new scale in order to get an accurate reading as he continued his diet.

Rob's story can tell us many things, not least of which

is that a dieter should not rely on an old scale! More important, though, it tells us something about the emotions we feel toward our weight. From our many conversations with others either wanting to or in the process of losing weight, it has become apparent that, more often than not, those with a weight problem would rather not face the reality of what they weigh. They share Rob's temporary anguish in coming to terms with how much he actually weighed. Thin people clearly feel no such anguish and thus are more likely to know their weight. Rob's sister-in-law and brother-in-law certainly did.

So, without further ado, buy yourself a reliable scale and get into the habit of weighing yourself every day. It should be the first thing you do every morning. The next time you reach for that bag of chips, whatever motivation you had when you started your diet will likely be forgotten in that moment of weakness, but the number you saw on the scale that morning, whether or not it was good news, will be shining brightly in your mind, reminding you to put down the chips and walk away. It worked for us, it's worked for friends and colleagues; there's no reason it can't work for you.

THE LAST LINE OF DEFENSE

Behavioral economics is critical in explaining why our number one behavioral best practice—the daily weigh-in—works. But it's important to add that this burgeoning field of economics has many more ideas to offer to the world of dieting. We'll a share a few of them in the remaining part of this chapter and many more throughout this book. But it's important to stress now that all of them are geared toward helping you develop habits—rather than just relying on willpower—that encourage healthy eating and help you combat the ever-present temptation to snack. By ingraining these habits in your day-to-day lifestyle, you will find it second nature to take into account your long-term health when deciding what to eat at any given moment.

Dan Ariely, a professor of psychology and behavioral economics at Duke University and the author of *Predictably Irrational: The Hidden Forces That Shape Our Decisions*, argues that the more decisions we have to make, the more likely we are to succumb to temptation. For example, an individual has a better chance of saying no to a chocolate cookie on one occasion than on ten occasions. Ariely therefore advises that we set rules for ourselves in advance—what he calls "meta-rules"—that cover all situations.[4] For instance, we could have a rule that allows us to eat dessert only on Friday night. One could think of this meta-rule as an oath we make to ourselves, a promise to avoid temptation no matter the circumstances.

This all makes perfect sense, and we fully endorse this advice. We also acknowledge that some meta-rules are more powerful than others. Committing yourself to salad every day for lunch will help because so often it is in the process of choosing lunch each day that the bad option becomes too tempting to ignore. Removing the agony of choice can help a lot. Yet, promising yourself that you will eat dessert only on Friday night will not magically remove the temptation to eat dessert every other day of the week. The oath we make to ourselves doesn't protect us from having to make a decision; it just changes the decision from "Shall I have dessert tonight?" to "Shall I break my oath tonight?" For sure, the latter holds more sway over us than the former, but it's not 100 percent foolproof.

Try These Meta-Rules

- Unless it's a special occasion, never have seconds.
- During the week, always have whole grain cereal for breakfast.
- During the week, always have salad for lunch.
- Always opt for the smallest portion of food or drink available.
- Eat out only once a week.
- At business lunches, order only a salad or fish entrée.
- Never eat more than two-thirds of what's on your plate.

The daily weigh-in, on the other hand, is powerful precisely because it arms dieters with information they can use to inform every eating decision—information that can overcome the temptations of the present. As we said, it is the tool that busts through the tunnel vision of hunger.

Fundamentally, though, we agree with Dan Ariely's

overall perspective: in a world of temptation, it is all too likely that we will succumb to present pleasure at the expense of future well-being. Even though these meta-rules won't be a panacea for your dieting struggles, we highly recommend experimenting with them because the more moments of temptation you can eliminate from your life, the better.

Despite both us having lost the excess weight years ago, every day is a battle against temptation and the desire to eat more food than is good for us. But having started the ritual of the daily weigh-in, we now have countless examples of times when knowing our current weight helped us combat the impulse to eat that unhealthy snack, ice-cream dessert, or second helping. Even so, there are moments that stand out for us, specific moments that enabled us to stay on the straight and narrow.

Dieting, as we have said, is not easy. Keeping the weight off, unfortunately, is equally tough. While Chris has maintained a healthy weight for well over ten years now, there have been a couple of occasions when he has come close to returning to his bad old habits. One particularly trying period came just after he got married, roughly three years after starting his diet and eighteen months after reaching his target. Spanning a Christmas during which he was fed enormous quantities of food by his new mother-in-law and just after his honeymoon to Argentina, Chris ate to his heart's content. Anyone who knows Argentina will know that the restaurants in Buenos Aires sell the best steaks in the world at the most ridiculously low prices. You just can't help but overindulge. Chris will forever remember one particular lunch as the "two-steak lunch." We don't think we need to tell you how it got that name.

During the honeymoon, and later while staying with his wife's family, Chris didn't have access to a scale. This proved disastrous. He knew he was gaining weight—he could feel it—but without the scale, it was impossible to gauge exactly how much he was gaining. Without the daily reminder that he was overeating, it was impossible for him to refuse temptation. So why not have that second steak? Especially at those prices!

When he finally returned home after six weeks, Chris was shocked to see that he had gained ten pounds. It was annoying and frustrating because he knew exactly what was required to get rid of that extra weight, having previously lost it. Putting himself back on a self-imposed austerity eating program certainly didn't seem appealing at first. In fact, he questioned whether he should even bother or just accept his new weight as the norm.

Chris Says

Even now, more than ten years after I started my diet, without my scale I seem to lose the ability to control my eating. Fortunately, digital scales are cheap! On more than one occasion, when I've been staying with family and friends and there's no scale in the house, I have bought them one. It's a peculiar thank-you gift, I admit, but it does lead to some interesting conversations. And best of all, you know there'll be a scale there that you can use the next time you visit. Failing that, when I've stayed in a vacation rental home (often on the Outer Banks in North Carolina), I've taken a scale with me! Of course, most hotels that have even a rudimentary gym also provide a scale, so there's no real excuse for not using it. But if that's not an option, a couple of fellow dieters have told me that in lieu of a scale, they kept on track by using a tape measure on their waist every day.

But the number on the scale helped him put his weight gain into context (he'd regained only about 20 percent of the weight he'd lost) and strengthened his resolve. In short, it made all the difference and got him back in gear. While on vacation, he had reverted to eating on autopilot, but the daily weigh-in had jolted him to attention. He returned to his habit of getting on the scale every day and lost the weight within two months. The daily weigh-in had provided the last line of defense between his natural proclivities to overeat and his better judgment.

Though Rob has been fighting the battle of the bulge for far fewer years than Chris has, he's also fallen off the wagon a handful of times during periods when he was unable to weigh himself regularly. This typically happens on extended vacations when he doesn't have access to a scale and—because he's away from his daily routine—is generally less vigilant than he would be otherwise.

For anyone who doesn't believe you can gain ten

pounds in two weeks, all you need to do is follow Rob on his annual pilgrimage to North and South Carolina. His wife's family hails from Denver, North Carolina, a small exurb near Charlotte nestled along the shores of Lake Norman. The trip always includes as much homemade Chex Mix as his mother-in-law can shovel into his face; she literally makes buckets of the stuff. Rob estimates he eats 5,000 to 10,000 calories' worth of Chex Mix alone on a typical trip. And when he and his family aren't gorging on homemade snacks, they're probably chowing down at the Bar-B-Q King or another local favorite. (Another piece of advice: if you want to lose weight, stay out of southern restaurants—or just the South in general. As a proud southerner, Rob knows that the food from where he grew up is delicious—though quite often terrible for his waistline.)

Rob's parents live in upstate South Carolina. In a pinch, Rob's hometown of Simpsonville could stand in for Dillon, Texas, in the television series *Friday Night Lights*. It's a land of chain restaurants, Walmarts, and, of course, high school football, in which America's obesity epidemic is on full display. Like many towns in the South these days, Simpsonville is littered with a local brand of Tex-Mex restaurants. We've already established Rob's weakness for Tex-Mex, and during his trips home, he can be counted on to consume copious amounts of tortilla chips, nacho cheese dip, and steak fajitas.

Like many other people we've talked to, at the end of a typical two-week visit to his beloved family, Rob can easily weigh ten pounds more. This, by the way, is no exaggeration, even though it flies in the face of many studies showing that over a festive period such as Christmas, the average person gains only about one pound.[5] Frankly, having monitored ourselves for many years and spoken to many people about weight gain, we think there must be something wrong with these studies. After all, in America, the overindulgent season begins in late November with Thanksgiving, and year-end celebrations with colleagues, friends, and clients seem to start on December 1. Our experience accords with the findings of the British Dietetic Association: "Over the festive period, which seems to kick off earlier and earlier every year, the average person could consume an extra 500 calories per day, equating to a weight gain of around 5 pounds by the time we reach the beginning of the New Year."[6]

After his Christmas trip home at the end of 2014, it took Rob nearly two months to lose the ten pounds he'd gained and return to his preholiday weight. In January and February, it was painful to slowly watch the pounds tick off once he had returned to more austere eating habits. Without the scale as a daily reminder of his Christmas excesses, the chances of dropping the weight again would have been much lower. Just as it was for Chris, Rob's daily meeting with the scale provided the necessary jolt out of eating complacency that we can all slip into so easily.

Still don't believe that weighing yourself every day is the surest way to dieting success? A growing body of research backs us up. A team led by doctors Carly Pacanowski and David Levitsky of Cornell University published research in the *Journal of Obesity* in 2015 indicating that frequent self-weighing is an effective tool for losing weight and keeping it off.[7] Their study of 162 overweight adults[8] didn't prescribe any particular weight loss regimens beyond stepping on the scale each day. "It used to be taught that you shouldn't weigh yourself daily, and this is just the reverse," Levitsky remarked about their findings. The scale, he theorized, "acts as a priming mechanism, making you conscious of food and enabling you to make choices that are consistent with your weight."[9]

Levitsky's comments really get to the heart of the matter. In chapter 3, we will return to the discussion of the daily weigh-in and explain how the scale can be used to experiment with one's own body, enabling the dieter to make better eating choices. But the key takeaway here is that the daily weigh-in helps a dieter cut through the narrow and confused thinking associated with the hunger that comes with self-imposed eating austerity.

Of course, you could wait for nutritional scientists and psychologists to find more conclusive evidence, or you could just see for yourself. If you don't own a scale, go out and buy one immediately. Your daily weigh-in—and your first step forward on the path toward weight loss—can start tomorrow morning. If you start now and record your weight loss journey, you too could have a chart that looks like this:

Rob's Weight Loss in 2014 (Pounds)

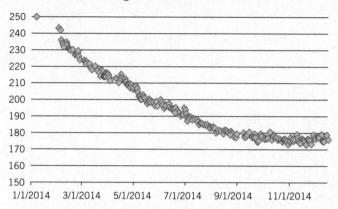

Key Behavioral Best Practices
Explained in This Chapter

CORE MICROHABIT

- Weigh yourself every day.

ADDITIONAL MICROHABITS

- Listen to your body's signals of hunger and fullness.
- Wait before satiating hunger.
- Seek moral support from friends and family.
- Establish meta-rules to guide future decisions about what to eat.

CHAPTER 2

ABUNDANCE

(Busting the Myth
of Three Square Meals a Day)

Losing weight and keeping it off requires restructuring your daily routine so that you eat less. Part of this routine, as we discussed in the previous chapter, is to weigh yourself daily so that you have a constant reminder to stay on track. But the second step—and the next core behavioral best practice we recommend in the Economists' Diet—is to let go of the routine of eating three *square* meals a day.

During our weight loss journeys, we have discovered that a person needs only one square meal a day, supplemented by two lighter meals, to stay satiated and healthy. We define a square meal as one containing less than half, but more than a third, of your daily recommended calories (explained in depth below), which is the rough equivalent of a six- to eight-ounce serving of protein and two vegetables. At the same time, we've also found that we are eating traditionalists. Sticking to three set mealtimes a day is a good way to avoid snacking and overeating. For us, eating more frequently but in much smaller quantities—a fashionable approach to weight loss known as "grazing"—just increases temptation. After all, each time you break bread is another opportunity to fall off the horse.

In this chapter, we will delve into the history of American eating habits to explain how the three-square-meals-a-day routine came about—and why we are arguing that only one meal should be square. But we also want to place these habits in the context of the broader challenges that abundance poses, both economically and culturally. After all, our daily eating routine is one facet of living in a world in which all too often we have our cake and eat it too.

WHAT IS A SQUARE MEAL?

There are many problems one can face in life—death, destruction, disease, and myriad other unpleasantries—but abundance isn't usually considered one of them. Indeed, we are the first to recognize the irony in the fact that the microhabits we advocate as part of the Economists' Diet are designed to help people defeat their own gluttony, while so many others exist in a state of forced starvation. Meanwhile, those of us who struggle (or have struggled) with our weight often complain about the state of our bodies while failing to do anything about it—even though (unlike those who are starving) it is entirely within our power to do so.

Chris's lunches at McDonald's back in the day were a

ABUNDANCE

classic example of this paradox: he would whine to his brother about how he needed to do something about his weight while simultaneously chomping down on a super-sized Big Mac meal topped off by a cheeseburger dessert. And let us not forget that this book would not exist if Rob hadn't complained to Chris about getting fat, all the while sensing that his weight reflected his own proclivity and ability to eat out whenever he wanted.

Our point is that it's better to accept the problems that come with abundance and do something about them than to continue feeling deeply unhappy about your weight. As you have read, we ate what we wanted when we wanted it—lots of snacking, of course, but mostly we became used to and expected to eat three full-sized, or square, meals a day. If we set aside calorie-laden drinks, a typical day looked a lot like this:

What Not to Do		
	Chris	**Rob**
Breakfast	Beans on toast	Breakfast burrito or a bagel with cream cheese
Snack 1	Chocolate	Chips

75

	Chris	Rob
Lunch	Lasagna or a burger—with fries, naturally	Sandwich from a local restaurant with fries
Snack 2	A cookie or three	More chips
Dinner	Pasta with a nice dessert and drink	Various restaurants, five or more nights a week!

If this doesn't define abundance and overconsumption, then what does? We understand, of course, that the vast majority of people who live in rich countries don't have enough money to buy anything they want whenever they want it. But when it comes to food, there are many millions who are pretty close to this point, given their personal preferences and tastes. They, too, enjoy eating three square meals a day.

A square meal could be

- Pancakes with a side of bacon for breakfast.
- Grilled meat—say, six to eight ounces in weight—with two vegetables on the side. (By vegetables, we don't mean French fries, or, for that matter, any potato-based side dishes.)
- Grilled fish and a side of Brussels sprouts or spinach.
- Grilled cheese sandwich and a small bowl of tomato soup.
- Spaghetti Bolognese, heavy on the sauce, light on the pasta.
- Something that's filling but not a gut-busting splurge!

A light meal could be

- A salad, perhaps including three to four ounces of grilled meat.
- A small bowl of soup. Try lentil soup if you haven't already; it's low in fat but full of healthy nutrients, and best of all, there's a ton of recipes online. Alternatively, enjoy a small helping of homemade Bolognese sauce without the spaghetti.
- A half portion of leftovers from last night's dinner.
- A plate of grilled vegetables.

For some, overeating is facilitated through snacking, but for us, while we did snack too much, the number one factor was our desire—always satisfied—to eat three square meals a day. It was through this routine that abundance precipitated overeating. By weighing ourselves every day, we came to realize that we needed only one square meal a day, with other meals made up of lighter fare. Two or more square meals a day equal too much food.

Try This Now

Get a tape measure and see how large your dinner plate is. If it is more than nine inches wide, try using a smaller plate or a shallow bowl instead.

According to Alex Bogusky's book on US consumerism, *The 9-Inch "Diet": Exposing the Big Conspiracy in America*, since 1970, the average American dinner plate has grown from 9 inches in diameter to 12 inches. Using the famous formula we learned at school—area of a circle = πr^2—that means that the area of a standard dinner plate has almost doubled, from 64 square inches to 113 square inches.

The classic example of a square meal is, as we have said, a six- to eight-ounce serving of protein (generally meat, though if you're a vegetarian, this could include tofu, beans, lentils, or a similar food) and two vegetables (or a salad). As a rule, we recommend no more than two side dishes because the more elements there are to your dinner, the bigger it's likely to be. And if you're eating a dish that includes a combination of food types, such as lasagna, then you shouldn't be adding sides at all. For us, a "square" portion of a casserole is roughly a four-by-four-inch square (five, max, if the bake pan is shallow). To give another example, if you're eating fish tacos, as Rob often does, then two tacos are enough for a square meal, and again, no sides are required.

If you've had a square meal for lunch, then breakfast should have been no more than a bowl of cereal, and you should have something light for dinner, perhaps soup or a salad. Bear in mind, a broth with chicken is light, but a thick chicken soup with cream and pasta isn't; likewise, a salad that includes a heavy dressing, croutons, and lots of other fixings. Our preference, given that we like to sit down and eat dinner with our families, is to have a salad for lunch and our square meal of the day for dinner. More often than not, our square meal doesn't include dessert; however, if you've taken a second helping, then dessert is definitely off the menu. As a rule, a square meal does not involve two plates of food, a second helping, or dessert; if there must be one of either, it should be tiny. When we are conscientious enough to make our portions small—in other words, they definitely don't fill a normal-sized 12-inch dinner plate—then there's room for dessert, such as a piece of fruit or a half cup of ice cream (not a half pint).

In order to determine how heavy or light your meal was, pay attention to how you feel after you've eaten. If you're satiated but you could eat more, then your meal is probably square; if you're stuffed, then your meal has crossed over into splurge territory. In short, a square meal is filling but won't make you pat your tummy afterward and groan, "Man, I'm full."

We appreciate that some readers may be looking for a more definitive measure of a square meal. As such, we offer the following calorie-based definition of what constitutes a square meal and how it differs from a light meal or a splurge. While distinguishing between meal-size types is an art rather than a science, one that comes with much practice and the use of a scale (in chapter 3, we caution against counting calories as a weight loss technique), we would say in general that a square meal contains less than half your normal calorie intake but more than a third. Following this logic, a splurge is a meal containing more than half your normal daily intake of calories; a light meal, less than a third. Some numbers should help illustrate the point.

Let's assume a daily calorie intake of 2,500. (The United States Department of Agriculture [USDA] has estimated the number of calories needed by a moderately active adult male of average size aged between eighteen and sixty-five to be 2,550.[1]) A square meal tops out at around 1,250 calories (half your daily intake), as this number of calories implies enough room for two lighter meals: say, one of 400 calories (most likely breakfast) and one of 700 calories, leaving a further 150 calories for tea and coffee and some fruit. Any meal over 1,250 calories is necessarily classified as a splurge because of the difficulty involved in finding a meal below 400 calories. Once you get to a 1,600-calorie meal (for instance, a large burger and fries washed down with a couple of beers), just to stay within 2,500 calories for the day allows (again assuming tea, coffee, and fruit of 150 calories over the course of the day) for eating only one other meal of no more than 750 calories, which is still light by our definition. In other words, by virtue of the math alone, a 1,600-calorie splurge will require you to skip a meal just to stay within your daily calorie limit.

For the average adult female, needing only 2,000 calories a day, a square meal tops out at around 1,000 calories. Assuming 100 calories of drinks and snacks, and breakfast of 400 calories, one maximum-sized square meal (1,000 calories) leaves room for only another meal of 500 calories, light by anyone's standards.

Examples and math aside, the truth is that knowing what a square meal is ultimately comes with practice, not formulas; and appreciating this point is essential to fully understanding a core message of the Economists' Diet: *so long as you're permanently relying on someone else to tell you what represents overeating and what doesn't, then you'll never truly have your weight under control.* Only by weighing yourself every day and connecting your behavior with your weight will you begin to develop an understanding of what counts, for you, as a square meal that is concomitant with successful weight management.

It was only through weighing ourselves every day, for instance, that we learned that grilled meat and salad is a square meal, whereas pizza represents a splurge. And while this may sound suspiciously like nutritional advice coming from two economists, it's important to realize that we came to these conclusions only by following our own microhabits so assiduously. Specifically, by weighing ourselves every day, we have been able to conclude that a carb-heavy dinner, like pizza, will lead to weight gain; grilled meat and vegetables won't. To know what a square meal is requires you to go on the same journey. Assuming that you can lose weight only as long as you have a manual telling you what to eat at all times or providing a rigid definition of a square meal is, in reality, the same as giving yourself an excuse for inaction.

To sum up, a square meal allows you to have two lighter meals over the course of a day; a splurge leaves room for only one other meal. (And some splurges are so large that you shouldn't eat anything else at all that day!) Yet acknowledging these limits and sticking to them is another matter—and clearly a problem for many living in rich countries around the world, where we are witnessing an epidemic of obesity and weight gain that threatens our future well-being. The problem is one of abundance, and that problem is unlikely to disappear on its own. If you want to change your body, you will need to self-impose eating austerity. It's time to start a new eating routine that includes eating only one square meal a day.

THE CULTURE OF ABUNDANCE

Saying this is all very well, but a large part of the problem is that overeating habits have become ingrained in our psyche, doing nothing for our long-term health. Looking back, we, Rob and Chris, realize we'd just gotten used to eating so much that we never questioned what we were doing; it all seemed entirely normal. Indeed, our expectations for eating each day were just one facet of a lifestyle—made possible by ever-increasing economic abundance—that reflects a culture which accustoms countless millions to satiate their every desire *right now*.

For many, including us, slower economic growth and large budget deficits since 2008 haven't changed much about the way we live our lives. We are still ensconced in a consumer-driven world where we expect to be able to get whatever we want without having to wait too long. This is especially true when it comes to eating, as there has been no marked deflation of our waistlines. We may have tightened the reins on our consumption in the wake of the initial financial meltdown—for instance, personal savings rates in the United States increased from 3 percent in 2006 and 2007 to 6 percent from 2010 through 2016[2]—but, in general, frugality is not part of our way of life.

Abundance and entitlement have rendered waiting unnecessary, and, for many, it has become unacceptable. When we're hungry, the idea of holding off until the next meal—let alone skipping the meal altogether—

is considered ridiculous. It goes without saying that the snack industry has been very successful in exploiting this. Think, for instance, of those entertaining Snickers ads that tell you "You're not you when you're hungry" and should therefore satiate that hunger with a Snickers bar as quickly as possible. Worse still, in an attempt to utilize our desire to manage our weight in their sales efforts, food companies have taken to labeling many snacks as "low calorie," as if that somehow makes snacking a good thing.

Surely the best thing to do if you want to stay healthy is not snack at all. In which case, avoid them whenever possible. Don't take them to work and don't keep them at your desk. And, of course, bringing your own lunch from home is the best way to avoid walking into restaurants, sandwich shops, and other food stores during the day that are packed full of unnecessary snacks and treats. Any tactic that helps you avoid being in close physical proximity to snacks, keeping them out of arm's reach, is one we'd heartily applaud.

Losing weight and keeping it off require eating out less. (We have a lot to say about this later.) But setting up your kitchen in preparation for self-imposed eating austerity provides a perfect opportunity to witness the culture of abundance in action.

Up to this point, we have asked you to purchase two things: (1) this book and (2) a scale. For now, what other equipment should you buy? Most likely, you have all of what you need already.

Here's our list:

1. a good set of knives,
2. a couple of cutting boards, and
3. a couple of pots and pans.

And that's about it, really. In fact, we recommend buying as little equipment as possible.

Ultimately, you are going to have to prepare more food for yourself at home. Packaged food from grocery stores and food from restaurants are often stuffed full of weight-gaining calories and other unhealthy ingredients such as salt and preservatives. By preparing your own meals, you will do yourself a massive favor by being able to control exactly what and how much you eat and just generally being more knowledgeable about what you're putting in your body.

Naturally, our consumerist culture has facilitated a whole host of kitchen appliances—from juicers and soup machines to steamers and yogurt makers—designed (at least in theory) to help you live a healthier life. If you genuinely enjoy using these products, then by all means buy them. (Rob's daughter, Ramona, loves fresh apple juice, so the two of them delight in a homemade glass two or three times a week.) But do not think for a second that you need them to lose weight. Spending money on this stuff is, more often than not, a way to avoid—and even exacerbate—the real problem at hand: overconsumption.

The British have an expression, "All the gear, no idea," that describes the impulse we all sometimes feel to rush out and buy a bunch of stuff when trying something new; and it aptly describes how many consumers prepare for a new hobby or activity. Consider the number of brand-new golf clubs or skis currently collecting dust in garages around the globe; or that shiny treadmill or exercise bike that now serves as a clothing rack or storage facility despite your original belief that having the equipment in your home would magically compel you to exercise more.

The same concept of "All the gear, no idea" is particularly present in the kitchen, which is so often packed with barely used state-of-the-art stoves, cookware, and specialized gadgets for slicing, dicing, and spiralizing. Upmarket kitchen stores make a mint, and you're left with a bunch of stuff you neither need nor use.

The root of this problem is the belief that we can transform ourselves into something we're not (for instance, sportsmen or chefs) by buying as much equipment as possible. But one does not become proficient at something simply having all the tools of the trade; what is required instead is hard work, practice, and dedication. You can't buy your way to becoming a good cook or a decent golfer, just as you can't buy yourself thin.

The good news is that you'll need to cook only one square meal for yourself a day, so you'll actually need even less equipment than you think! And as you'll read later on in chapter 5, we are great believers in simple cooking, so you won't need to be Bobby Flay or Mario Batali to whip up something satisfying.

Understanding our second core behavioral best prac-

tice—to eat one square meal a day instead of three—requires a change in mind-set, an acknowledgment of the role that our culture of abundance plays in facilitating and encouraging us to expect more than is reasonable. Whether dealing with kitchen equipment or the food we are making with it, we need to expect and accept that less is better.

FORGET THREE SQUARE MEALS A DAY, ONE IS ENOUGH

Learning to eat with intention instead of on autopilot is one of the key messages of the Economists' Diet. Over time, we, Rob and Chris, got fat because our eating habits and routines came to drown out the signals (hunger and fullness) that our bodies were sending us. The most pernicious of these habits was eating three square meals a day. Regardless of how empty our stomachs were, we sat down and ate our next large meal at the same time every day simply because we had formed the habit of doing so. This had to stop.

Some of you may be wondering whether what we are saying is reasonable. How can we be expected to live if we don't participate in a quintessential human routine that has been practiced for centuries? Consider two important points: first, "Thou shall eat three meals a day called breakfast, lunch, and dinner" is not a commandment carved in stone from some all-powerful being up on

high; second, and more important, the notion that ɛ
meal should be square, or full-sized, is a modern inve
tion made possible by our age of abundance.

What do we mean by eating on autopilot?

- Grabbing a snack when you're not hungry. Remember: always listen to signals from your body.

- Automatically buying something like a croissant or chocolate bar to go with a cup of coffee, instead of ordering just coffee.

- Grabbing a donut or bag of chips when you fill up your gas tank. (Interesting aside: many gas stations make higher margins on food sales than they do on the sale of gasoline.)

- Walking mindlessly into Taco Bell instead of the salad joint next door.

- Taking second helpings.

- Finishing off your kids' dinners, only to sit down later to eat with your spouse.

- Filling all the space available on your large dinner plate with food.

Try This Now

The next time you eat, be mindful of what you're eating while you're eating it. This means:

- Don't multitask while eating. Your primary focus should be your food and who you're eating with, not your TV or smartphone
- Slow down your eating and savor each mouthful. Eating should not just be about shoving a bunch of food down your gullet because you're hungry, invariably eating more than you need.
- When eating with others, respect the meal as a social ritual taking place around a table. Talk about the food you're eating.

To be sure, we do not expect you to either want to or be able to unilaterally spurn your eating timetable. Sitting down and eating food with spouses, partners, children, friends, and colleagues at specific times of the day is part of our culture; it's not going away, nor do we think it should. Enjoying a meal together is one of life's pleasures and is essential for interaction and general conviviality.

All we are saying is that, if you choose to eat a good helping of spaghetti Bolognese for dinner, then breakfast and lunch should be light: a small bowl of whole grain, nonsugary cereal for breakfast (don't be fooled by cereals packed full of sugar that market themselves as a "great source of whole grains") and a salad or something similar for lunch. If you want to eat a hearty sandwich (and most sandwiches these days are hearty) and a bag of chips for lunch, then you have to accept that as your one square meal for the day. Breakfast that morning should be light—for instance, a small bowl of cereal or a soft-boiled egg with one piece of toast (no pancakes or waffles, fried eggs, sausages, bacon, and so on)—and dinner should be very modest: say, a salad with a very limited amount of protein, such as a half palm amount of chicken, roughly 4 ounces in weight.

Chris Says

When I was obese, nothing gave me more pleasure than a large breakfast. The "full English," with bacon, sausage, beans, hash browns, and a fried egg, was a particular favorite. Now I've made a habit of having a bowl of whole grain cereal every day. This raises eyebrows: Aren't breakfast cereals meant to be the devil, full of sugar and carbs? For me, I've found a bowl of healthy cereal to be filling and entirely commensurate with weight loss. But there are two golden rules:

1. It has to be a *small* bowl, not a bucket!
2. Check the nutritional information. In addition to being whole grain, the cereal you eat should have no more than 5 grams of sugar per 30-gram serving. Unfortunately, you may have to do a little math here. Some cereal manufacturers play around with the standard serving sizes in order to

make their products appear healthier than they really are. I have seen one cereal state that it has 9 grams of sugar per serving of 27 grams, compared with another cereal showing 9 grams per serving size of 55 grams. While both disclose 9 grams of sugar, assuming the same serving size, the former actually has twice as much sugar as the latter.

In coming to terms with this, we think it's helpful to look beyond Western and modern conceptions of mealtimes for a little perspective. For instance, when European explorers of the sixteenth and seventeenth centuries encountered tribal peoples in North America, they soon appreciated that Native Americans had no real eating routine at all. According to explorer John Smith, one of the founders of the first permanent English settlement in Jamestown, Virginia, in 1607, they had "no such thing as set meals, breakfast, dinner, or supper."[3] Instead, they ate when hungry. Like many societies studied by anthropologists, there were no standard mealtimes; in response to signals of hunger, snacking, often on the move, provided relief. This way of eating was punctuated by rare bouts of feasting, often forming part of a ritual. While we definitely don't recommend a similar approach, we'd wager that snacking like this would be fine so long as you are eating unprocessed foods such as an apple or a few carrot slices!

Nor should we assume that the three-meal-a-day routine started with the rise of "civilization." Ancient Romans, for instance, opted for one square meal a day—at lunchtime—and actively frowned on eating in the morning. This tradition was carried over into the Middle Ages, as the Catholic Church criticized eating before morning mass. By the time people were allowed to eat, they really were ready to "break the night's fast."[4]

Clearly we are not asking you to pretend you are a citizen of ancient Rome (though that might be fun for other reasons) or to behave like our premedieval forebearers—though some popular meal plans these days do champion a diet that would be consistent with this. We are simply trying to make the point that what we take as a set-in-stone ritual that all humans have shared for all time is anything but. Our eating customs are relatively new.

Even though we don't condone eating three square meals a day, we are proponents of eating at three set *times* a day. For instance, from observing our own behavior and its effects on the scale, we've accepted that snacking is something we need to avoid so long as we choose to eat breakfast, lunch, and dinner. If we could always limit a snack to a single piece of fruit, it might not be so problematic, but experience has taught us the stimulation we get from snacking usually means that one Dorito leads to another. Generally speaking, snacking is bad and should be avoided, and eating at regular times helps us avoid snacking.

We should add that we're not anti-snacking zealots. A lawyer colleague of Chris's wife, who was seeking advice on weight loss, pointed out that she couldn't make it past eleven in the morning without a granola bar. Hunger pushed her to distraction, so, she asked, what was she supposed to do, given that at twelve thirty she went to the cafeteria for a square-sized lunch with colleagues? Chris suggested that if she really couldn't have a productive morning without a small snack—preferably an apple or other piece of fruit, or perhaps a few almonds or walnuts, as opposed to the carb-and-sugar-laced granola bar—then she should eat a smaller lunch to compensate. Meanwhile, by stepping on the scale every day, she could monitor how her new diet affected her weight and could figure out, over time, what sized lunch was best. Simple and obvious advice, yes, but this individual was so fixated on her inability to give up the snack that it had not occurred to her that it wasn't necessarily the need to snack that was causing her to gain a few pounds but rather what she was snacking *on* combined with the square lunch that followed.

As we said, we, Chris and Rob, are creatures of habit, and regular eating times help us avoid overeating. For us, regular means three times a day. We don't subscribe to diets that recommend more frequent and smaller meals: for example, eating five or six small meals a day, in what is often called grazing. First, eating so frequently exponentially complicates diet planning because it requires you to pay greater attention to what you put in your mouth on any particular occasion. And second, any eating habit that brings us into contact with food more often is a bad idea. We need to stay away from temptation as much as we can.

There's little doubt that eating three times a day is a natural complement to the contemporary lifestyle of anyone living in the industrialized parts of the world. It also has a long history. According to the Yale University historian Paul Freedman, a peasant living in medieval Europe "would start his morning with ale or bread or both, then bring some sort of food out into the fields and have a large meal sometime in the afternoon . . . He wouldn't have a large evening meal. He would just grab something small and quick."[5]

Abigail Carroll's history of American eating habits, *Three Squares: The Invention of the American Meal*, explains that European settlers landed in the United States with a similar eating routine (save, perhaps, the early-morning beer). The main meal of the day was taken in the early afternoon, with leftovers often recycled for light meals in the early morning and late evening. "Breakfast and supper featured fare whose main function was to keep the stomach satisfied until the next decent filling," she writes. "Often the morning and evening meals were glorified snacks."[6] Until well into the nineteenth century, a large proportion of Americans ate pottage—a thick soup or stew made by boiling a variety of vegetables and meat—as their main meal and the leftover pottage at other times of the day. Yum!

Not only did the main meal take place around noon but also this once-a-day square meal was called dinner, signaling that people dined at noon but ate relatively lightly in the morning and evening. It was only during the latter half of the nineteenth century that dinner migrated from noon to six o'clock. The change in habits reflected both fashion and practicality. Rapid urbanization and industrialization and the formalization of business practices during the latter half of the 1800s required workers to travel greater distances during the day. This disrupted the centuries-old pattern of working locally—most commonly on the land where one lived—that had enabled families to gather around a table for dinner at noon. With workers traveling relatively large distances to work, dinner had to move to the early evening to enable the family to continue to eat together once a day.[7]

With dinner now at sixish, lunch had to be invented, as people needed a midday meal that would provide them with enough sustenance to keep working until dinner. Luncheon clubs sprang up for the more affluent, and women of the leisure class imported fanciful ideas from afternoon tea rituals in Europe—especially France. For the masses, bread tended to form the basis of the new American lunch. Later, the second industrial revolution around the turn of the twentieth century—which utilized technological enhancements to machines to rapidly scale up production—brought about a burgeoning industry of restaurants specializing in selling lunch, whether in separate establishments or in lunchrooms within factories and office buildings.[8]

By the mid-nineteenth century, the first meal of the day

had become very substantial indeed, coming to resemble what we would today consider a standard hot breakfast: eggs, sausages, beefsteaks, cold meats, baked goods, and porridge. Often these meals were large because they provided the energy necessary for early-morning hard labor. With changing work practices, these habits were leading to rising health concerns. The door was left open for entrepreneurial spirits to transform breakfast into something healthier, as they had lunch. The most famous example is of course the Kellogg brothers—both vegetarians—who used ideas developed by health reformers such as Sylvester Graham, another vegetarian and inventor of the original sugar-free graham cracker. (Note: the original Kellogg's Corn Flakes, invented by John Harvey Kellogg in 1878 and still popular today, lacks the copious amounts of sugar now added to many cereals you find on grocery store shelves). In short order, breakfast cereal became a testing ground for the latest developments in food manufacturing and packaging, as well as for new promotional and advertising techniques.[9]

For our purposes, the key takeaway from this fascinating history is that modern eating habits developed alongside the emergence of modern cities and factories, with their attendant transportation and infrastructure networks that enabled workers to travel longer distances every day. The three-meal-a-day routine was perfectly adaptable, and entirely appropriate, to the needs of the workers during the second industrial revolution; for example, think of Henry Ford's car manufacturing facilities, which required strict adherence among its workers to a rigid daily schedule. In particular, three square meals a day was the perfect complement to the efficiency of the factory floor. The urban existence of the worker, an entirely revolutionary way of living, required a new way of eating. Our modern eating rituals, then, are no more than 150 years old.

The wide acceptance of the three-square-meals-a-day formula, coupled with improved efficiencies in the industrial process, accelerated in the twentieth century; while two world wars created a need for the government to jump on the bandwagon. Three proper meals at set times of the day enabled large companies and the government to plan and control output better. Such a dietary regime ensured that workers had enough energy each day to be sufficiently productive.

The West grew rich through manufacturing advances, and, thankfully, agricultural production was able to keep up with the demands of a growing population that needed more sustenance and could afford to pay for it. The eating regimen that has become so ingrained in our culture was the perfect complement to ever-expanding wealth generated on the production line. Moreover, it's probably fair to say that eating three square meals a day was healthy given people's daily activities at the time. In Britain, for instance, even with rationing during the Second World War, people continued to eat three square meals a day of a better nutritional standard than is generally eaten today. It was a critical part of the war-winning effort.[10]

THE ECONOMISTS' DIET

America and other rich nations are no longer the manufacturing powerhouses of the world. Yes, there are millions of manufacturing jobs left in the West, but many of them involve supervising robots rather than hard physical labor. And far more people work in the service sector and in offices, where they simply don't expend the same amount of energy as those on their feet all day. So many of us drive to work, sit at a desk, work long days, drive home, sort out the kids, and then go to bed, making it difficult to burn that many calories and maintain our weight. The average worker in the postindustrial West uses significantly less energy than their industrial predecessors did, while at the same time, food processing and higher incomes have created opportunities and temptations to eat more than we ever have.

Rob Says

I spend roughly nine hours a day at my desk—my employer is kind enough to provide "standing desks," so I alternate between sitting and standing. I typically arrive at work around eight in the morning and stay until six, with an hour break at lunch. By the time I get home at six fifteen, I've got roughly two hours to eat a quick dinner, give the kids a bath, get them ready for bed, and read them bedtime stories. On a good night, the kids are in bed by eight—or nine thirty on a bad night—leaving little time for much else, and certainly no time for physical activity.

ABUNDANCE

> My hectic day is why watching what I eat is so impor-
> tant: when you're this busy, it's so easy to take your eyes
> off the ball. Managing what you eat is one of the few
> things you can actually control.

Customs, traditions, and their attendant habits of thought are very sticky and tend to survive long after their reasons for being have disappeared. We take it for granted that we should eat three square meals a day, yet that routine no longer makes sense. Abundance is making it virtually impossible to maintain such habits without putting on weight. Sure, sit down and enjoy three meals a day, but only one of those mealtimes should be "square."

STOP MAKING EXCUSES

It's so easy to find an excuse as to why you're overweight. At some point, you've probably blamed your body's particular metabolic structure or convinced yourself that having eaten too many carbohydrates has rendered you permanently prone to being overweight. You do this not simply because you're in denial (though you probably are) but also because autopilot eating prevents you from seeing the impact of your own behavior. As this chapter shows, we pay far too little attention to how automatic overeating is tied to cultural norms. And with any path to recovery, the first step is to admit you have a problem.

At the start of his weight loss journey, Rob begrudgingly arrived at this conclusion after a stern conversation with Chris. "Believe it or not, I'm actually one of the thinnest people in my family," Rob said. "What I'm saying is that I'm fighting an uphill battle. Controlling weight isn't something that comes naturally for my family. We struggle with it." Rob had honed the excuse that he was fat because of his genetic predisposition, not because of his behavior. In fact, by his own logic, he was doing quite well compared with his relatives. But as Chris pointed out, you can either spend time making excuses or invest that energy into losing weight.

Americans, in particular, are full of excuses regarding their waistlines, and they're coddled by an army of dietitians, weight loss experts, and authors who want to blame almost everything but behavior. Think your metabolism is to blame? More likely, it's the bag of Doritos you just ate.

Most diets tend to find a central culprit: it's not your fault; you're just eating too much sugar, too much bread, too many carbs, too much saturated fat. The list goes on and on. While clearly there are exceptions and complicating factors, we prefer to follow the philosophical maxim known as Occam's razor, which holds that if there are two explanations for the same phenomenon, with one being more simple and one more complex, the simpler one is usually correct.

The simple answer in this situation is that if you're overweight, you're eating too much food. You therefore need to eat less. This should be intuitive, but it's not; that's why we've provided some examples in this chapter of what constitutes a square meal and what a lighter meal should look like. There's much more on this in chapter 5.

Of course, our leading health experts regularly uncover additional factors that remind us that eating less is easier said than done. As already mentioned, a study published in the journal *Obesity* in 2016 followed former contestants from the hit TV show *The Biggest Loser*.[11] In another of the researchers' findings, nearly all of the show's contestants have regained a significant portion of the weight since they appeared on the show, and the study determined that metabolism was to blame.[12] According to the authors, your body fights efforts to lose weight— possibly because our hunter-gather physiology makes our bodies see weight loss as a sign of impending famine and a signal to build up reserves—and adjusts your metabolism accordingly. They concluded, therefore, that formerly obese people have a naturally slower metabolism than those who were never overweight in the first place. Yet another bit of cruel irony provided by Mother Nature.

While we don't dispute the study's scientific findings, it still strikes us as an excuse. Neither of us have had our metabolism measured, so maybe they are slower than they were before we got fat. Either way, we have figured out how to work with the bodies we have and have accustomed ourselves to eating an amount of food that will not cause us to gain weight. As an aside, we wouldn't recommend rapid weight loss like the sort championed on *The Biggest Loser* anyway. Your body needs plenty of time to adjust to new habits—such as eating only one square meal a day—so, as frustrating as it can be, losing weight should take time.

How much you eat, not what you eat, is the problem. The evidence for this is overwhelming, especially once we look outside the United States to other countries in which abundance has collided with ingrained cultural patterns to increase waistlines. Chris lived for two years in Kuwait, a country that now suffers from a higher rate of obesity and diabetes (by population) than the United States. To some extent, it's easy to see why this is so: the country is packed full of every North American restaurant chain under the sun. Standing in the middle of the Avenues, the largest shopping mall in the country, you can turn around and see Shake Shack, Starbucks, Cheesecake Factory, Tim Hortons, Elevation Burger, Potbelly Sandwich Shop, Texas Roadhouse, and Olive Garden. And that tally doesn't even include the host of European, Asian, and Middle Eastern restaurants that are also clearly visible in this single panoramic take.

The existence of these chains, all offering loads of carb- and sugar-laden temptations, has been made possible by the rapid increase in wealth that Kuwait has witnessed since large-scale oil extraction became a reality in the 1970s. In 2014 aggregate national income was around $150 billion, shared between roughly one million Kuwaiti citizens and two and a half million noncitizen residents. Gross domestic product per capita, which includes all residents, was around $50,000, very similar to that of the

United States, although the average Kuwaiti is substantially better off. Increasing abundance has gone hand in hand with an increasing incidence of weight gain. According to the World Health Organization, in 2014, 72.7 percent of Kuwaiti men eighteen and older were overweight, compared with 48.3 percent in 1975, when mass oil extraction was just starting.[13]

Knowing this, one might still argue that Kuwait's obesity problem is caused not by overeating but by eating the wrong things. After all, the restaurant chains mentioned above are hardly known for their healthy options. However, an understanding of the eating habits of Kuwaitis suggests that quantity really is the problem here, and the increase in quantity has come about precisely because traditional eating routines have been merged with, rather than displaced by, Western restaurants.

We can imagine that many people reading this book don't know an awful lot about Kuwait, except that it's in the desert and very hot. Knowing this, however, is actually a good starting place from which to understand our point. Largely because of the heat, the average Kuwaiti workday starts and ends early; the standard day is seven thirty to two thirty. There is no lunch break so that workers can get home and continue the Kuwaiti tradition of sitting down to a large meal with their families at three in the afternoon.

Traditionally this three o'clock nosh made for Kuwaitis' one square meal a day. Yet while Kuwaitis continue to eat lunch with their families, the arrival of so many restaurants has led them to adopt a new habit of socializing in the evening by eating out. They have, therefore, in the span of a few decades, gone from having one large meal a day to having two. No wonder Kuwait suffers from some of the highest obesity rates in the world.

There are all sorts of excuses one can make about weight gain, but sometimes we have to just let them go and accept that we have been overeating. This was the case for Rob and Chris, and while it may not be universal, it's a truth shared by many around the world. Kuwait provides an ideal case study: a country that has experienced rapid increases in wealth followed by the rapid onset of an obesity epidemic. The smoking gun is not the kinds of foods Kuwaitis are eating (although that is not helping) but the fact that their adoption of Western eating habits, including a restaurant culture, has doubled the number of large meals they consume per day.

Our microhabits apply way beyond the shores of the United States. Chris has explained his ideas not only in his native England but also in Kuwait. Locals there showed great interest in the Economists' Diet precisely because it was so relevant to their recent environment of abundance. Chris's Kuwaiti colleague Ali lost twenty-four pounds in six months following our recommendations and has kept the weight off ever since. While he cut down on rice and fatty meat, key to his success was giving up dinner, or at least limiting it to eating a few dates (a delicious Middle Eastern alternative to an apple). He realized that as long as he wanted to achieve lasting weight loss, eating a square-sized dinner was incompatible with his family meal in the afternoon.

Chris also had detailed discussions about Kuwaiti eating habits and diet with a fairly well-to-do Kuwaiti woman. This thin woman was a perfect example of our point about how thin people behave differently. Throughout her adult life, she has weighed herself every day and even gone so far as to take a photo of the number on the scale each day and send it to her sister (who, to be honest, admitted being rather tired of receiving the photos) for moral support. To many, she was naturally thin; in reality, Chris's Kuwaiti friend was fastidious about measuring, monitoring, and managing her weight. We have much more to say about the use of data in weight loss in the next chapter.

Key Behavioral Best Practices
Explained in This Chapter

CORE MICROHABIT
- Eat one square meal a day.

ADDITIONAL MICROHABITS
- Learn to identify meals as either square, light, or a splurge, and manage your daily intake accordingly.
- Spend money on kitchen essentials, not on fancy equipment you'll never use.
- Keep snacks out of arm's reach; better still, resolve not to buy them in the first place.
- Stop making excuses for why you're overweight.

CHAPTER 3

DATA

(Be Calorie Conscious, Not a Calorie Counter)

Over the course of our professional careers, we have been involved in many situations that have required us to gather and interpret data. When confronted with a new question or problem, or in order to test a new hypothesis, we hope that by seeking out empirical, fact-based information (data) and analyzing it to identify trends and patterns, we can explain what has happened in the past and make educated predictions about what may happen in the future. When we do our jobs well, we can use all of our newfound wisdom to suggest policies and programs that will (hopefully) make a difference for the better.

In the process, we have learned how data can be used (and abused) and, critically, that some data sources are more reliable and user-friendly than others. When clear, complete data are available, and you know how to interpret and apply it correctly, the data can illuminate truths and clarify solutions to problems that may have previously seemed insurmountable.

Data, at its best, helps plug information gaps between what you know and what you don't know, signaling the need to alter habits or ways of thinking in order to improve outcomes. Just imagine how frustrating it would be to buy shares on the stock market without financial information about these potential investments. In a similar fashion, data have played a critical role in our respective weight loss journeys, helping us to measure progress, change our behavior, and manage our route to our goal weights.

The best example of this is the daily weigh-in, but if you've tried other weight loss programs, you may be familiar with another type of data collection: calorie counting. This is the practice of tallying the calorie content of everything you eat throughout the day in order to ensure you don't surpass your recommended allowance. The logic behind this makes sense on the surface: if you know how many calories you should be consuming, then all you need to do is keep track of what you eat throughout the day and stop eating once you've reached your limit. But while we have learned through experience that calorie data can—like the daily weigh-in—be an extremely powerful tool in helping us make better choices, we don't recommend that you count every last calorie. Instead, we propose a more sensible and more time-saving approach to using calorie data, which involves being what we call "calorie conscious."

MAKING BETTER CHOICES
BY BEING CALORIE CONSCIOUS

If you type the maxim "If you can't measure it, you can't manage it" into Google, you'll discover a wealth of discussion and disagreement about who said it first and exactly what it means. Peter Drucker, possibly the most famous and influential of all business management gurus, is frequently credited with the saying, but Drucker also understood that, in any organization, if you've got the wrong people and the wrong culture, no amount of data is going to ensure the right outcome.

Our professional lives have been a testament to "If you can't measure it, you can't manage it." But we also know that price data don't always provide all the information we need to make better decisions. Our obesity epidemic reflects this conundrum. In one important respect, it has come about because of a market failure, defined by economists as a situation in which the fundamentals of supply and demand don't account for unexpected costs, known as negative externalities—for instance, think of environmental damage caused by underregulated petrochemical plants. The production revolution has led to cheaper processed foods, but the low prices of these foods fail to account for the costs to our health later on. Nor, for that matter, does the price of cheap junk food incorporate the cost associated with being forced to buy larger clothes when we've gone up a size.

Consumers can use calorie information, especially when eating at restaurants, as a tool to correct this failing. To explain this, we need to consider what prices, as data, enable us to do when they do their job properly, and then think about when prices may be sending us the wrong information.

Austrian economist Friedrich Hayek provided the finest explanation of prices as signals in a famous 1945 essay called "The Use of Knowledge in Society." The best way to summarize Hayek's thesis is by sharing a (possibly apocryphal) tale that Chris once heard. As the story goes, the mayor of Moscow paid a visit to London in the late 1980s, just as the Soviet economy was slowly falling apart toward the end of the Cold War. Once in London, the mayor noticed that no one had to queue up for bread. In fact, the supply seemed to provide everyone with enough bread at cheap prices, without wasted bread piling up on street corners. He was amazed and asked a British official how the government managed such an incredible feat of planning. How, for instance, were suppliers able to estimate demand so perfectly? How were daily and seasonal variations accounted for to ensure that there were no regular shortages or supply gluts? How, quite simply, did they price the bread?

The answer was, of course, they didn't. The government played no role whatsoever in the provision of bread. Knowing this only raises other questions. How, for instance, does a mom-and-pop store manage to supply bread so effectively? Surely such an operation requires a deep reservoir of knowledge, including the state of the wheat market, food processing techniques, supply logistics, and macroeconomic demand conditions?

In reality, mom and pop need no such knowledge. All they must know is how much their supplier is charging them for the bread. Soon thereafter, they'll find out how many loaves they sell each day and therefore how many loaves to buy from the supplier. Over time, they'll even learn if there are certain times of the year—holidays or the summer months, for instance—when fewer customers are around, and they can temporarily reduce inventory. Likewise, their supplier doesn't need to know the intricacies of the wheat market or the costs involved in producing bread: all that information is wrapped up in the price. According to Hayek, prices are signals that have the ability to contain and amalgamate the millions of pieces of information and knowledge required for us to coordinate our economic activities, without the need for large-scale planning. One look at planned and controlled economies versus market economies tells you that, on the whole, prices do a much better job than government does at bringing buyers and sellers together efficiently.

But sometimes things go awry. In the 2000s, it became fashionable for investors around the world to buy securities that gave them rights to receive mortgage interest payments from American home buyers. The prices of these securities suggested that all was well and that there was little risk these borrowers wouldn't pay back the loans. We all know what happened next: many of these investments turned out to be worthless, indicating that investors had not been privy to enough information to make an accurate assessment of the financial condition of the borrowers and the precarious state of the housing market. The underlying problem was one of what we economists call "information asymmetry," a condition in which one side of a transaction knows more about the product than the other. One of the reasons the crisis was so severe was because there were so many levels of information asymmetry. The banks originating the loan knew too little about the borrowers, and the investors buying into the loans knew too little about the structure of the securities they were buying.

All investment decisions suffer from information asymmetry. So what to do about it? Well, rather than end our market system and do away with prices altogether, regulators, like the Securities and Exchange Commission (SEC) in the United States, have focused their attention on increasing disclosure. Companies that are listed on Nasdaq (the National Association of Securities Dealers Automated Quotations exchange) or the New York Stock Exchange are required to release voluminous amounts of data every quarter to help investors make more informed decisions. The purpose of this data is to close the information gap between buyer and seller and enable prices to do a better job of capturing reality. In short, if the market's broken, disclosure is an attempt to fix it.

Unfortunately for dieters in the United States, the disclosure of data about food has significantly lagged behind the disclosure of data about stock-exchange-listed companies. While the SEC was formalizing disclosure rules in the wake of the 1929 Wall Street crash and ensuing Great Depression, the US Food and Drug Administration (FDA) started demanding nutritional food labeling only in 1990.

Even so, you may be justified in thinking that disclosing more data hasn't been that effective at solving the underlying information problems. After all, the hundreds of pages published every quarter on Lehman Brothers alerted almost no one to its impending doom in September 2008. And while the FDA was relatively late to the disclosure party, there is no indication that more nutritional data have improved people's eating habits; after all, as our charts in the introduction show, the proportion of Americans who are either overweight or obese has increased since 1990.

There are many reasons why more disclosure doesn't fix markets. Sometimes it's because the people using the data don't understand it, and sometimes it's because there's too much of it. Chris has been analyzing banks for over twenty years, but he still finds it difficult to make sense of the thousands and thousands of data points disclosed by the biggest banking institutions. The nutritional data listed on food packaging can be equally mind-boggling. People say nutrition isn't rocket science, but Chris's dad, a math graduate and retired information technology manager with type 2 diabetes, and therefore someone with a personal interest in deciphering nutritional data, admits that he finds the whole thing totally baffling.

The main problem is that most of it is noise. Do you really need to know what percentage of your daily recommended allowance of vitamin D you're getting from a serving of Oreos? No. On top of that, it doesn't help that nutritional scientists aren't always in agreement about what is good for you and what isn't.

Confused about what to eat and what not to eat? So are we: that's precisely why we focus on the daily weigh-in and keeping things simple. When it comes to nutrition, the oldest advice remains the best: eat lots of fruits and vegetables and eat everything else in moderation. But you knew that already.

Disclosure is not working as well as it should, and it doesn't take a rocket scientist (or an economist) to explain why. We all know intuitively that the best type of data is the stuff that is simple and straightforward. That's the point about prices. No one is overloaded or confused when they see that one loaf of bread costs $2.50 and another, fancier one costs $3.50. In short, we can make significant and effective changes to our behavior when good data are presented clearly and simply. When it comes to making eating choices, calorie information can be applied similarly.

In our search for microhabits that aid us in our daily struggle to control how much we eat, we have found that being calorie conscious, as opposed to calorie counting, is extremely helpful in making better decisions when buying prepackaged food or food from a restaurant.

As we shall explain in more detail below, while we

encourage you to use calorie data in certain circumstances as a tool for making better decisions, such as when a restaurant provides calorie data on its various meals, we do not advocate a regimen that involves calculating the calories in everything you eat every day. Indeed, we should point out that we, Chris and Rob, don't know the exact number of calories we should eat each day in order to maintain our respective weights. After all, some days we may burn more calories than others, and to some extent, we are all different, physiologically speaking. Fortunately, however, we don't need to know the exact number in order to use our calorie-conscious technique. Now, if we were calorie counting, we might care more about pinpointing this exact number so we could be sure we weren't surpassing it. But for a variety of reasons, including the daily grind of recording the calories we ingest, or the near impossibility of actually measuring the calorie content of everything we eat—issues we'll discuss in more detail in the next section—we don't think you should bother with calorie counting.

The best way to explain our concept of calorie consciousness is by providing an example:

Around the corner from our office when we worked together in Washington, DC, there was a very popular sandwich shop called Così. (Apologies to Così for singling it out, but the point we are about to make applies to every other sandwich/salad shop in the world that discloses calorie data on each item in the menu.) For the sake of argument, let's imagine that one of our female colleagues decides to buy her lunch there, and assume that she orders a salad and a piece of the (admittedly delicious) flatbread that comes free on the side. She opts for the signature salad, a combination of mixed greens, gorgonzola cheese, dried cranberries, pears, pistachios, red grapes, and sherry shallot dressing. This, she assumes, is a healthy, low-calorie option. After all, it's salad! A salad with *three* different fruits in it! However, before going ahead with the order, she needs to take a closer look at the calorie data provided by Così on its menu. It turns out that the salad, including the dressing, contains 662 calories, and the complimentary flatbread adds another 214. This brings the total calorie content of the meal up to 876.

Following USDA estimates that a moderately active adult woman, aged 18 to 65, needs, on average, 2,000 calories a day (1,967 to be exact),[1] we can see that this salad and bread lunch would provide her with around 45 percent of her daily calorie intake. It therefore qualifies as a square meal, as we defined it in the previous chapter. Okay, fine. But here's the rub: without checking the data on calorie content, our colleague could be excused for thinking that she was having a light lunch. Given that she may well consume 500 calories during the day, what with breakfast, drinks, and fruit, then dinner is going to have to be light, that is, contain under a third of her recommended daily calorie intake.

We would bet that many people miscalculate this

way every day, thinking that, surely, having a salad (or another similarly "light" meal) at lunch means you have room for a large dinner. Often, it doesn't. And this is precisely why we need to use data in our quest to maintain or lose weight. We have lost count of how many times our decisions have changed after looking at one simple data point—the calorie content on the side of a package or on a menu.

Perhaps more than anything, being calorie conscious has transformed our coffee-drinking habits. Chris's grande white chocolate mocha at Starbucks (400 calories) has been long since replaced with a caffè Americano with nonfat milk (no more than 30 calories). Indeed, if there is one rule that being calorie conscious has spawned, it is this: *do not drink your calories.*

Few people consider how many calories they consume when choosing what beverage to accompany a meal. But high-calorie drinks can wreck a diet, and they are all too available. Here are some ideas about how to substitute unhealthy drinks with better alternatives.

Drink	Calorie Content	Replacement/ Solution	Calorie Content
Grande caffè latte, whole milk (from Starbucks)	220	Grande Americano with nonfat milk*	30
Grande white chocolate mocha, whole milk (from Starbucks)	400	Grande Americano with nonfat milk*	30

THE ECONOMISTS' DIET

Drink	Calorie Content	Replacement/ Solution	Calorie Content
Venti mocha Frappuccino with six pumps of mocha syrup and whipped cream (from Starbucks)	490 Note: each additional pump of syrup on top of the basic recipe adds another 25 calories.	Grande Americano with nonfat milk*	30
12-ounce can of regular Coke	140	Soda water	0
Glass of red wine	85	Go for it! You've earned it!	85
Pint of beer	204	Glass of red wine?	85
Three pints of beer	612	Enjoy yourself! You only live once! Just don't pair it with pizza, burgers, fries and chips; or be prepared to self-impose strict austerity eating the following day (which may be difficult if you're nursing a hangover).	612

Sources: Starbucks, USDA
* Yes, you read that correctly. We believe in the power of habit. Rather than face an agonizing choice every time you order a coffee, stick with one type that is low calorie. That's what we both learned to do. Not only is the temptation to order anything different gone, but we've come to appreciate much more the real taste of coffee.

As economists, we are all about measuring and managing. The big issue is ensuring that you are measuring and

.anaging data that is concise and delivers an effective
,ay to change your behavior. Being calorie conscious will
improve your choices while ensuring that you never suffer
from information overload.

While the rules on disclosing calorie information vary
hugely from state to state, we are delighted to report that
the US Food and Drug Administration made it manda-
tory by the end of 2016 for all restaurants with more than
twenty outlets to make the calorie content of each product clearly available. The FDA took its lead from places
like New York City and the state of California, which
have had similar requirements for many years. For us,
this small government intervention is a victory for common sense. Sure, there are studies out there that question
whether publishing calorie data on menus leads to better
decision making,[2] but we reckon the problem stems from
people not knowing what to do with the information. By
being calorie conscious, we can quickly and easily incorporate one piece of information into our decision making
to change behavior for the better.

DON'T COUNT CALORIES

Calorie consciousness is a coping mechanism to avoid
overeating by signaling relevant data that help us resolve
regular occurrences of information asymmetry. Hopefully
by using the data, we end up being nudged toward a bet-

ter choice. But clearly, for calorie conscious
effectively, the dieter has to make it a pereni
check calorie data when available. This is easie
certain places than at others. For example, larg
rant chain menus often list calorie counts, but th
diner might not. Even so, once you start to acquire ca
information, you'll become more knowledgeable ab
how many calories are contained in certain food item
even if you don't know the exact number. The same goes
for ready-to-eat food bought in grocery stores. One look
at the calorie content of a pint of Häagen-Dazs or Ben
& Jerry's ice cream may inspire you to choose a sorbet
or a lighter flavor instead. That said, if you are anything
like us, it may not. When eating ice cream, we'd rather
enjoy the good stuff, using calorie data—assuming we can
face looking at them—to direct us toward making these
creamy delights a rarer treat.

Rob Says

I often don't have time to pack my lunch for work; fortunately for me, there's a salad-only restaurant called
Chopt a couple of blocks from my office. And because
the restaurant lists the calorie content of each salad next
to the price, I use this information to help guide my decision. While I enjoy the chain's Texas Po'Boy salad (680
calories) and its Classic Cobb (670 calories), I gravitate
toward the menu's lower-calorie options: Kale Caesar
(290 calories) and the Mexicali Vegan (360).

There is, however, a fundamental difference between a nudge that comes with being calorie conscious and counting calories, which presupposes total control.

Calorie counting is also a method that aims to resolve the information asymmetry that exists between buyers and sellers of food. The difference is that calorie counting is far more ambitious. Calorie consciousness is focused on buying ready-to-eat food most often prepared outside the home. Typically, we are thinking of sandwiches and salads bought for lunch and drinks bought throughout the day, though it could apply equally to microwave or premade meals bought from the grocery store; what matters for this technique is the disclosure of calorie data. Calorie counting, on the other hand, is very tough because it is nearly impossible to calculate the calorie content of food you make yourself.

Calorie counting aims to leave no stone unturned; to know exactly how many calories you are ingesting over a certain period of time. The dieter is permanently accounting for everything she eats and using the data to work out what to eat at each meal. The calorie counter is not using signals to compel her toward better decisions but is focused instead on total planning and control. Without overstating the parallel, we think that rather like a communist government trying to plan and control a complex economy, calorie counting fails because it's too difficult to measure and manage such a large array of data. It is, in short, an unsustainable (not to mention stressful) approach to weight loss. Sure, you may succeed in losing weight in the short term by following such a rigorous method, but unless you're one of those self-quantification nerds who likes to monitor everything going on with his or her body at any given time, we're willing to bet that the pounds will creep back on once you've ditched the practice.

The practical difficulties of strict calorie counting seem insurmountable to us. Anyone adhering strictly to such a regimen would most likely have to lock themselves away and prepare every single thing they eat themselves. This is neither desirable nor realistic. Then just think of the burden of trying to record each calorie consumed. Unless you're collecting calorie data continuously throughout the day, you'll never be able to perfectly recall every meal and every snack you ate and how many calories they contained. You'd potentially have dozens of entries per day, especially if you were including coffee and other drinks. Even as economists, we start to balk at the size of the spreadsheets you would need to keep track of all the data.

On top of stress, our most serious objections to rigorous calorie counting have to do with measurement error and data frequency. Even if you were able to obtain precise calorie information for all the food you consumed, you'd still be missing the other half of the equation that determines how you gain and lose weight: metabolic rates and calorie expenditures reflecting exercise, other physical activities, or just the energy used up from being awake and your body performing its basic functions (known as your basal metabolism).

Take the issue of measurement error. If you inadvertently underestimate your caloric intake by just 10 percent to 15 percent each day, you'd end up consuming an extra day's worth of food each week! Given that an apple can range from 53 to 116 calories,[3] it's not difficult to imagine how easy it would be to miscalculate one's caloric consumption by this magnitude. Even if you're eating packaged foods, there's good reason to be skeptical of the labels. A 2010 study by Lorien E. Urban and colleagues at Tufts University found that frozen foods from supermarkets contained an average of 8 percent more calories than advertised on their labels.[4] The same study found that restaurant-prepared meals had an average of 18 percent more calories than advertised.[5] With such unreliable data around, it's likely that even the most diligent calorie counter will regularly overshoot his or her daily target. Of course, that doesn't mean we recommend ignoring calorie data altogether, but findings like this suggest that our approach is more in tune with the nature of the data: it's an estimate rather than hard scientific fact. And the more you rely on calorie data, the more the measurement error will accumulate. Being calorie conscious two or three times a week is going to keep measurement error within sensible and reliable limits.

The practical and theoretical difficulties of calorie counting have, of course, spawned an entire industry ready to help us navigate the impossible data tracking required to do it ourselves. And it's no small industry: in 2015 Oprah Winfrey paid $43 million for a 10 percent stake in Weight Watchers, a weight loss program that instructs participants to keep track of their calories by using a highly curated system that assigns a point value to everything they eat.[6]

To be fair, Weight Watchers offers much more than the simple calorie counting we've described. Their program includes four pillars to its weight loss approach: a food plan (each dieter has a points plan, with points for certain foods allocated according to calories and other nutritional information), an activity plan, a behavior modification plan, and group support (weekly meetings that include having your weight measured). We certainly share the company's faith in behavior modification, although its approach is very different from ours.

Some people may assume that because a calorie-counting program like Weight Watchers relies so heavily on data, it is more "scientific" and therefore more efficient than our comparatively lax habit of calorie consciousness. But to us, it just seems like remarkably hard work. For starters, you have to measure every ingredient you use when cooking or eating—from the amount of milk you put on your cereal for breakfast to the number of almonds you munch on for an afternoon snack. What a hassle! And what about going out to eat? Unless the restaurant is going to reveal its nutritional information, you're back to guesswork, which could put you way off the mark. Strict adherence to calorie-counting routines or similar programs basically precludes you from going out for six months. You may lose the weight, but your social life will be kaput.

DATA

Even with all the difficulties that come with the heavy workload of managing and measuring your diet 24/7, Weight Watchers does have proven, though perhaps limited, success. A study published in the British medical journal *Lancet* in 2011 followed 377 volunteers who were enrolled in Weight Watchers for one year. Of the 230, or 61 percent, who completed the program, the average weight loss was roughly eleven pounds.[7] Still, over the long term, things are more difficult. A 2001 study in the *International Journal of Obesity* reported that only 19.4 percent of the 1,002 participants who finished the Weight Watchers program were still within five pounds of their goal weight five years later.[8]

What to Do with All the Extra Time You Would Have Spent Calorie Counting?

- Jog a mile or two or take a leisurely walk.
- Call your mom; we're sure she'd like to hear from you.
- Post something on social media about how many pounds you've lost. The positive feedback you're sure to receive from friends and family will be a great motivator to keep going.
- Spend a few extra minutes on your favorite hobby.
- Relax: read a book or watch a rerun of your favorite sitcom with a nice cup of tea. (No snacks!)
- Browse online for all the new clothes you'll need to buy once you've reached your target weight.

We have conducted a more limited survey among our friends and families. Among the people we know who have gone through calorie-counting diets, a few were able to reach their target weight over a designated period, but none was able to maintain the weight loss after having stopped the diet. One friend, Laura, lost around twenty pounds in twenty-three weeks back in 2011, but the weight crept back up, and by 2016, she was right back where she started.

Laura didn't hold a grudge; she appreciated that her strict calorie regimen had worked and that she had learned about healthier eating along the way. She also recognized that paying for weight loss advice had given her an incentive to follow it. "Having paid the money," she told us, "I would have felt like a bit of a twit for not losing weight." This, of course, is music to economists' ears: we love incentives! Laura also found the practice of weighing herself once a week as part of the program hugely motivational, yet she still ended up regaining the weight. Asked why, she blamed it on snacking. After our discussion, she accepted that a strict calorie-counting plan was simply impossible to continue forever. Once she left the program, there were no behavioral controls to keep her from snacking or overeating.

This doesn't surprise us at all. Almost by definition, any attempt to completely close the information gap between you and the food you're eating has to be draconian, encapsulating excessive planning and control. We are, perhaps oddly, reminded of Princess Leia's retort to Darth Vader in *Star Wars: A New Hope*: "The more you tighten your grip, the more star systems will slip through your fingers." The tighter the controls over eating practices, the more likely people will give up, returning to their old habits once the controls are released.

DIETING AS AN EMPIRICAL METHOD

Calorie information can help nudge you to make better decisions. Yet, as we've explained, while we recommend being calorie conscious as a core behavioral best practice of the Economists' Diet, we think calorie counting is fundamentally flawed. Does this mean that there is no way to close the information gap between what we eat and the effects on our weight? That there will always be information asymmetry between the producer and consumer of food?

No. But the information gap can only be closed over time. By weighing yourself every day, you will soon gain the necessary data and knowledge to connect the dots between your behavior and your weight. Before long, you will be able to measure and manage your weight with a high degree of precision—without driving yourself crazy or setting yourself up for failure in the long run.

So while we've already written about the power of the daily weigh-in to shield you against eating temptations, it's now necessary to stress the other critical role that the daily weigh-in plays in providing data. Once established as part of your routine, it's a habit that takes less than thirty seconds, compared with the several minutes per meal or snack it requires to record your calorie consumption. It is, to use another term from economics, more or less "frictionless" with regard to time: you can step on the scale each morning while brushing your teeth and not lose a second of productivity.

A core principle of the Economists' Diet is that a dieter needs to experiment with the foods he or she eats and how that translates to the scale the following morning. This will help you start to understand your body. Assuming that you maintain the same level of activity each day, you will begin to learn what food makes you gain weight and what food makes you lose it. Likewise, you will figure out what happens if you cut out this food and replace it with another item instead. Most of all, you will learn how much food is too much and how much is too little. By experimenting with your body, using data from the scale, you come to know exactly what changes you need to make to your diet in order to lose weight.

As noted at the start of this chapter, we are empiricists. If we have a theory, we like to test it out using data from the real world. If we believe, for instance, that oil prices rise and fall in relation to oil inventories in China and the United States, we want to test our hypothesis statistically with data. This is no different from an entrepreneur who tests her product on potential customers before bringing it to market and then responds appropriately to sales data and customer feedback after the product has been launched.

All of this is simply part of the scientific method. We are fully aware that in practice science can be messy, random, and driven by politics, culture, or a range of other factors. But in its ideal form, science is about testing, rejecting, and refining hypotheses. As the philosopher of science Karl Popper described it, science never ends because, ideally, scientists should always be designing experiments that try to disprove accepted theories.

We believe that dieting requires the dieter to turn himself into a nutritional scientist of his own body. Armed with only a scale, you can quickly discover all you need to know about what works and what doesn't: test your theories, modify your theories, and, if necessary, reject your theories.

Of course, this approach is based on one fundamental underlying assumption. As such, the following statement needs to be read carefully. *Our daily weight is unquestionably connected to our behavior.*

Among the pushbacks we've received against the Economists' Diet when describing it is that the daily weigh-in is a bad idea. "I hear you," many people struggling with their weight have told us, "but you're not supposed to weigh yourself every day. It's too frequent."

It's amazing how many people seem to believe this myth. Usually, folks will argue, "There's too much volatility in your weight, and an unexplained uptick might discourage you." But we just don't buy it. As far as we can see, the opposite is much closer to the truth. Not only is there no apparent medical or scientific reason to avoid the daily weigh-in, but our own experience has taught us that it is essential to keeping you on track. Chris has been playing this game for more than ten years and has learned so much about his body that he can pretty much predict what his weight will be the following morning based on what he's eaten the previous day. Using personal data and experimentation, he has, quite literally, solved the information asymmetry problem that exists between himself as a buyer of food and all his various food suppliers, whether they're restaurants or grocery stores. (Of course this hasn't stopped him from performing the daily weigh-in, but over the years, it has increasingly become a game in which he guesses in advance what his weight will be.)

One of the reasons we recommend weighing yourself each day is because it helps you detect patterns and connections. If you're weighing yourself each week, as many diet programs recommend, you're not being given the opportunity to see how each day's behavior affects your weight. More to the point, if you're weighing yourself each week, you're seeing the impact of twenty-one meals on your weight as opposed to three. The higher frequency makes it much easier to identify what works and what doesn't. You might find yourself swapping that "healthy" salad and flatbread lunch for a lentil or chicken vegetable soup.

Of course, we've learned a lot about what works well for us, and we expect that you, through the process of experimentation, will discover many new connections we hadn't considered. Weighing yourself daily won't always bring good news, but it should help you identify foods and behaviors that are particularly fattening. Forget the old aphorism "You are what you eat" and adopt our more accurate version: "You weigh what you eat." Once you've developed the habit of weighing yourself daily, you're going to have hundreds of opportunities to experiment each year.

Your behavior over short periods of time matters. If your numbers on the scale creep up several days in a row, then it's a sure bet you haven't been eating the right quantities of food for the prior few days. Most people probably know that leafy green vegetables are good for them and a burger and fries are bad for them; even in our world of abundance, we generally haven't lost sight of what *types* of food can cause us to gain weight. But without taking the matter into our own hands, we have lost the ability to gauge the right *quantity* of food we can eat without packing on the pounds. After all, an Iowa science teacher named John Cisna proved that you can lose weight eating almost anything, so long as you're eating it in sufficiently small amounts. As part of a scientific experiment for his students, the 280-pound Cisna ate nothing but McDonald's—breakfast, lunch, dinner—for a total of six months. Not only did he lose 61 pounds, but his "bad" cholesterol (known as low-density lipoprotein, or LDL) went down! [9]

When identifying the foods and behaviors that cause your weight to tick up, pay particular attention to things that cause you to gain two or more pounds. We've noticed that after a particularly gluttonous weekend, it's not unusual for us to have gained several pounds come Monday morning. For example, Rob gained four pounds over a long weekend in Austin, Texas, at his buddy Ian's bachelor party. He had a great time, and he ate plenty of barbecue and other rich foods. Rob wouldn't trade that experience for the world, but if he ate like that every day—lots of fatty meat, cornbread, macaroni and cheese, mashed potatoes, and so on—he'd be back on the road to obesity very quickly. It seems pretty intuitive that such foods, especially in large quantities, make you weigh more, but seeing the impact on the scale helps bring home the point.

Although *The Economists' Diet* is not a nutritional guide, let alone a cookbook, we want to share some of the key insights we've gained from experimenting with the scale over the past few years. While we primarily believe that your weight loss goal can be achieved by eating less of everything, we've also learned that carbohydrates such as breads, pastas, sugars, and potatoes are particularly problematic on the scale, pound for pound, compared with other foods, and so we recommend eating less of them. We'd encourage you to substitute leafy green vege-tables or other low-calorie foods for these carbs.

Try This Now

- Throw away all the chips in your home and resolve not to buy them again.
- Next time you are given a choice of sides in a restaurant, opt for salad over fries (unless it's a special occasion).
- Ban yourself from eating pizza for the next two weeks.
- Ban yourself from eating pasta for the next week.

When it comes to bread, we don't just mean the stuff that comes in a loaf. Bread encompasses everything from toast to hoagies, and from croissants to pizza. Tortillas and tortilla chips also count—a fact that is especially germane in the United States, which has become obsessed with Mexican food over the past few decades. The same goes for pasta. Basically, if wheat is the primary ingredient, then consider cutting back. With regard to sugar and potatoes, we're obviously thinking of more than a teaspoon of white sugar or an individual baked potato. Our list would include everything from soda and candy to cupcakes and some varieties of peanut butter, which contain large amounts of sugar, let alone fat. In addition to soda, sugar-laden drinks such as apple and orange juice are also problematic. As we've said already: *Don't drink your calories!* Anything with high-fructose corn syrup or other sugar substitutes also counts. And in the case of potatoes, of course, we're really thinking about items such as French fries and potato chips, the latter of which are really bad for the waistline.

Why are breads, pastas, sugars, and potatoes so bad? Because they produce what is called the glycemic response. In layman's terms, these foods cause your blood sugar (glucose) to increase, which basically tells your body to store fat. In other words, a certain amount of these foods is going to cause you to gain more weight than an equivalent amount of salad. Science and food writer Gary Taubes has written several excellent books on the topic, including *Why We Get Fat: And What to Do About It*, which we recommend if you want the lowdown on how carbs and other foods affect your body chemistry.

Even if Taubes hadn't meticulously catalogued the science of how your body responds to sugars and other carbohydrates, we expect you will arrive at the same conclusion by experimenting with your daily weigh-in. Here's a simple experiment to try: skip all breads, sugars, pastas, and potatoes for a day and observe what happens on the scale the next morning. If your starting weight puts you in the overweight or obese classification (see the next section), we suspect, just as we've observed for our own bodies, you'll see an immediate weight loss, perhaps even dropping an entire pound or two overnight. The following day, if you go back to eating these foods in the quantity you're used to, expect your weight to snap back up. For so many people, these foods represent a material proportion of their calorie intake, so if you cut them out, you'll be killing two birds with one stone: eating less stuff that has been proven to lead to weight gain, and eating less, period.

Remember Laura, our friend who used calorie counting to lose twenty pounds back in 2011, only to see the weight return once she stopped her strict regimen? Chris spoke to her in 2016 right after she had returned from her summer vacation in Italy. That day, she happened to be back at her highest weight and felt fairly downbeat about it. She wasn't planning on returning to strict calorie counting and control, but her mind was set firmly on losing weight.

To that end, she was weighing herself every day—she knew that much about the Economists' Diet—and had successfully lost one pound a day for two days running. But that morning, speaking to Chris, she was demoralized. According to her, she had "starved" herself the previous day only to see zero effect on the scale that morning.

Laura is a mom who works three days a week, traveling more than an hour each way to her office. The day before she spoke to Chris had been her first day back after her vacation, and she had been careful: a slice of toast for breakfast and a low-calorie salad for lunch. The train ride home had been a nightmare due to a strike across London that day, taking almost two hours, but even so, Laura had avoided the temptation to snack. By the time she got home, her husband had already fed their two daughters and put them to bed. While there was some leftover pizza in the fridge, Laura knew that pizza wouldn't help the weight loss, so she sat down and ate spaghetti with a Bolognese (tomato and meat) sauce instead.

There was silence on the phone. Chris pointed out that the pasta was clearly the culprit, and Laura realized that even though the spaghetti seemed so benign—after all, it contained no fried foods, and the sauce had been made with natural ingredients—it was making it more difficult for her to control her weight. As we've said, by experimenting every day with the scale, we have come to learn that a large dose of pasta for dinner will make weight control very challenging indeed.

In response to Laura's question about what she should have eaten instead, Chris suggested more of the nourishing sauce with only a little or perhaps even no spaghetti. More to the point, he went on to explain that weighing herself every day was only half the ticket. She needed to adopt an experimental mind-set: measuring the impact of different foods and different quantities on the scale, and opening up to the possibility that things she had eaten all her life were likely part of the problem.

No Pasta Required with This Delicious Chili Soup

Next time you feel like having spaghetti Bolognese, make this veggie chili instead. It is delicious on its own and serves between six and eight people. Alternatively, it can sit in the fridge for several days, supplying many meals to an individual or a couple. The recipe comes courtesy of a friend of ours.

1 tablespoon olive oil

1 medium onion, diced

2 cloves garlic, diced

1 tablespoon ancho chili powder

1 tablespoon paprika

1 tablespoon cumin

3 bell peppers (1 orange, 1 yellow, 1 red, or some combination thereof), cored and diced

1 can (64 ounces) tomato juice or V8

1 can (14.5 ounces) diced tomatoes

1 can (15 ounces) corn

1 can (4 ounces) diced green chilies

4 cans beans (15 ounces) (black, kidney, or pinto are best), drained and rinsed

Salt and pepper to taste

Heat the oil in a large soup pot or saucepan over medium heat. Add onion and garlic and sauté until fragrant. Add the spices (feel free to use more or less to taste) and stir until onions and garlic are coated. Add the bell peppers and sauté for 4 to 5 minutes, until softened slightly. Add the tomato juice, diced tomatoes, corn, green chilies, beans, salt and pepper, and any additional paprika, cumin, or chili powder to taste. Stir thoroughly and cook on medium heat until it begins to simmer. Reduce heat to low and simmer for 10 minutes before serving.

THE ECONOMISTS' DIET

For further guidance on this, take a look at the table below. At points during his diet, Rob kept a food diary while recording his weight each morning. We think it's fairly easy to see the links between what he ate each day and the amount he weighed first thing the following morning. For instance, austerity eating has a visible impact the next day, whereas pizza is bad, but its effects can be moderated by skipping a meal. The table also makes clear that you can lose a modest amount of weight over the course of a week and still eat good, tasty food.

Rob's One-Week Dietary Experiment with a Scale				
	Morning Weigh-in/ Reflection	Breakfast	Lunch	Dinner
Day 1	189.2 *First day back to work after a vacation during which Rob gained five pounds.*	Blueberry, yogurt, and milk smoothie, two cups of coffee	Caesar salad	Three chicken tacos with a side of rice and tortilla chips
Day 2	191.0 *Oh dear! Looks like Rob felt the need to comfort eat after his first day back at work postvacation, and you can see the effects on the scale!*	Two apples and a cup of coffee	Salad including lettuce, corn kernels, black beans, grape tomatoes, avocado, onion with light dressing	Miso soup, one homemade scallion pancake

DATA

	Morning Weigh-in/ Reflection	Breakfast	Lunch	Dinner
Day 3	188.8 *That's more like it. Day 2 was definitely an example of austerity eating.*	Blueberry and milk smoothie, cup of coffee	Burrito Bowl from the fast-casual chain restaurant Eatsa (625 calories)	Homemade tamales and a few pretzels
Day 4	187.8 *Another strong performance on the scale after a day of light eating.*	Bowl of Cheerios, cup of coffee	Skipped lunch in preparation for family pizza night	Four slices of takeout pizza, a few garlic bites, salad, three amber ales
Day 5	189.0 *To be expected after the pizza and beer the night before. It would have been worse had Rob not skipped lunch.*	Cup of coffee (no food)	Lunch at Chinese restaurant: kung pao chicken, salt-and-pepper shrimp, side of rice	Spinach salad
Day 6	188.6 *That's okay. Skipping breakfast and keeping dinner very light enabled Rob to have a tasty lunch out and still shed almost a half pound.*	Two eggs, one slice of bacon, one slice of toast, cup of coffee	Apple	Pork chop and bok choy with soy sauce and other seasonings
Day 7	187.0 *Heavy on the austerity at lunch and lightish dinner paid off handsomely.*	Banana, yogurt, and milk smoothie	Mexican Caesar salad at Chopt	Small portion of homemade fried rice and an apple

TARGET SETTING, OR HOW MUCH WEIGHT DO I NEED TO LOSE?

Data collection, measuring, and managing is great, so long as you know where you're coming from, where you're going, and that you are plotting a realistic journey for yourself. In other words, you need to know what you are trying to accomplish by weighing yourself every day and being calorie conscious. In theory, an economist would tell you to go on dieting until the dissatisfaction of passing over the last piece of food you could have eaten is equal to the satisfaction gained from shedding the last pound.

Hmm . . . Good luck figuring that out, let alone reconciling all those different emotions!

Back in the real world, we know that for weight loss to be successful, you need to have a clear and precise goal in mind—what we call a target—to keep you motivated and moving forward. The art of target setting, be it short term or long term, is to make your end goal achievable. It's all well and good for an internet start-up to set its sights on market dominance when no one else is selling the same product. But if it's entering a market in which it will have to fight for its share with a number of competitors, it'll be setting itself up for failure—no matter how much data it collects—because its target is unrealistic. The worst kind of targeting we've seen—all too often, unfortunately—happens when someone sets a target with absolutely no clue of how to achieve it or even a sense of what data would be most useful to track the journey toward achieving it.

Telling yourself that you just need to lose "a lot" of weight is not precise enough. That's why our microhabits must go hand in hand with a clear and realistic weight loss target. We'll discuss what that means below, but we also need to stress up front that being realistic also means setting a doable time frame. In the next chapter, we explain why hoping to lose all your excess weight in a short burst is a fool's errand that will set you up for long-term failure. If you want to lose around fifty pounds or more and keep it off, you're better off thinking in terms of an eighteen-month timescale. Of course, to help along the way, we suggest setting intermediate targets. For instance, big round numbers make for good signposts—220 pounds, 210 pounds, 200 pounds, and so on—but don't take your eyes off the long-term prize. If you do that, you're far less likely to achieve it.

Chris Says

When I started dieting back in 2004, I'd been overdoing it so much that just replacing the lunchtime lasagna and fries with a salad or low-calorie sandwich was enough to get me started. I lost fifteen pounds in two months.

But after that, it gets more difficult, and things slow down. The more you lose, the more you're going to have to cut out of your diet to continue to lose weight. That's why after having lost fifteen pounds fairly quickly, it still took me another sixteen months to get to my target weight, for a total weight loss of forty-five pounds. Things slowed down because the changes I made to the way I ate needed to be sustainable and also because there were periods of feasting (holidays and vacations) during which I gained back a few pounds. If I had rushed the diet, as I had done during previous attempts to lose weight, I never would have developed the necessary habits that enable me to go on eating less in a world full of temptation. I surely would have regained the weight pretty quickly.

Weight loss is a marathon, not a sprint, to use the cliché. You need to be realistic. If you're, say, eighty pounds overweight, of course it's going to take a long time. But in our experience, it's entirely achievable.

We believe that the simplest way to set your weight target is to use the body mass index, also known as BMI. This is an easy calculation—which we will explain in a moment—that you can use to gauge how overweight you are and to calculate how much weight you need to lose. The BMI makes the assumption that the taller you are, the more you are likely to weigh; thus any estimate of where you stand on the normal-overweight-obese spectrum has to be based on your height. For instance, intuitively, assuming all three men are forty years old and weigh two hundred pounds, we can gauge that a five-foot-seven man is *obese*, a man who stands six feet tall is *overweight*, and a six-foot-four man is *normal*.

DATA

The BMI calculation is remarkably straightforward. The standard method is to take your weight in kilograms and divide it by your height in meters squared (that is, your height multiplied by itself). If you are working in feet, inches, and pounds, divide your weight in pounds by your height in inches squared (1 foot equals 12 inches) and multiply the result by 703. An even simpler way is to type the words "body mass index calculator" into Google and use one of the many online tools available to do the math for you.

A normal BMI range is 18.5 to 24.9. (Anything under 18.5 is considered underweight.) You're classified as over-weight if your BMI falls within the 25-to-29.9 range, and obese if it's north of 30. A BMI above 35 classifies you as severely obese, while anything over 40 is considered morbidly obese. Maybe you have already made the calculation yourself or had a friendly doctor make it for you. Either way, if you're reading this book, we'd venture to guess that you're not all that pleased about the result.

We can relate. Back in January 2004, when Chris had his fateful meeting with the scale, he weighed 220 pounds. Given that he is five foot ten (70 inches), his BMI score was 31.6 [(220 ÷ (70 × 70) × 703 = 31.6]. Ten years later, in January 2014, Rob went through the same exercise and discovered he had a staggering BMI score of 36.9!

Try This Now

Calculate your body mass index!

> Weight in pounds ÷ [(height in inches) x (height in inches)] x 703 = BMI

Here are three examples:

Man 1: weight 200 pounds, height 67 inches (5 foot 7)

67 x 67 = 4,489
200 ÷ 4,489 = 0.044553353
0.044553353 x 703 = 31.3 BMI

Man 2: weight 200 pounds, height 72 inches (6 foot)

72 x 72 = 5,184
200 ÷ 5,184 = 0.038580247
0.038580247 x 703 = 27.1 BMI

Man 3: weight 200 pounds, height 76 inches (6 foot 4)

76 x 76 = 5,776
200 ÷ 5,776 = 0.034626039
0.034626039 x 703 = 24.3 BMI

So, at the start of our respective diets, both of us were obese; and with a BMI of nearly 37, Rob was technically severely obese. Of course, we didn't need to calculate our BMI score to know that we had to lose weight; we just had to look in a mirror. But there is nothing quite like seeing those numbers and knowing that the medical profession has categorized you as obese to motivate you to start losing weight. It's not a good feeling, but it certainly brings home the reality of the situation.

We also know that the BMI is not a perfect measure. While one can overplay bodily differences by using them as an excuse for being overweight in the first place, we accept that everyone's body is unique. The BMI doesn't take into account any personal physiological characteristics when assessing your condition, such as natural body shape or the amount of muscle that a person has. So we don't use it blindly. But ultimately the BMI is one of the most straightforward ways to frame an individual's weight problem. Target setting is better than no target setting, and in this regard, we know of no better or simpler way to set your target.

Back to the point at hand: now that you know your BMI (if you haven't calculated it yet, we'll wait right here while you do so . . .), how many pounds do you need to lose to get to a healthy weight? Whatever your starting point—a BMI of 27 or 37—we believe a dieter is best off targeting a BMI of 25: the upper limit of the "normal" category. Why only 25? Because we are realistic! We're two middle-aged men, each with young families, and we both work full-time. We haven't got time to make our bodies "perfect," and these days, we don't even have the inclination. The days when we dreamt about wooing the ladies with our sculpted torsos and rippling biceps are long gone, and, more to the point, we actually enjoy eating far too much to focus all our time and energy on becoming lean, mean, data-crunching machines. It's just not a priority for us—nor does it need to be for you.

Our only goal when we started our diets—and this is our hope for you—was to lose enough weight so that we would no longer be technically overweight and could establish a sustainable base from which to lead a relatively healthy lifestyle without having to deprive ourselves 24/7. For all our concerns about overconsumption, we like eating a lot—after all, that's how we both ended up obese in the first place. We're not going to torture ourselves to get a BMI of 20. Sure, having a BMI between 22 and 24 would be great, but a BMI of 25 (or 24.9, to be exact) is entirely respectable, and it sets a target that is challenging without being impossible to achieve.

That said, there are plenty of people already in the normal range, with a BMI somewhere between 20 and 25, who still want to lose the ten to fifteen pounds they've gained in the past few years. For instance, one friend of ours wanted to get back to the weight she was before she had children, even though her current weight put her firmly in the normal BMI bracket. The good news is that everything we've said in this chapter (and, for that matter, in the rest of this book) can be applied to anyone who wants to lose weight, regardless of his or her starting point. If you are in the normal bracket and, for whatever reason, you wish to lose ten pounds, then clearly you don't need a BMI target; your target is ten pounds. Even so, be realistic.

Work out what your BMI will be at your desired weight; if it's under 20, ask yourself whether it's worth the pain. And cut yourself some slack: while you may have gained a few pounds over the past few years, you've almost certainly gained wisdom and perspective, too.

The final stage of target setting is to translate a BMI score of 25 back into a target weight so that you can figure out how much weight you need to lose to meet your goal. Using inches and pounds, rearranging the formula, we get:

$$\text{Target weight} = 25 \times (\text{height} \times \text{height}) \div 703$$

Let's use Chris as an example. He started off with a BMI score of 31.6, and his target score was 25. Using the rearranged BMI formula, his target weight was set at 174 pounds, meaning that he had to lose 46 pounds ($70 \times 70 \times 25$, all divided by 703 = 174.3 pounds. $220 - 174$ pounds = 46 pounds). Following the same approach, Rob needed to reduce his weight by 75 pounds to reach a target BMI of 25. Rob and Chris are about the same height (5 foot 10), so for each of them, the tipping point between normal weight and overweight is about 174 pounds.

As should be clear by now, we did it. And while you won't see us in a Calvin Klein underwear ad anytime soon, a BMI of 25.0 has been sufficient for us to feel better about our bodies and be healthier in general: lower blood pressure and lower cholesterol, just for starters. Because we set realistic targets, we were able to achieve our goals. Had we set a loftier goal by, say, refusing to rest until we looked like Thor, we'd have raised our chances of giving up early on and returning to our bad old ways.

That said, it wasn't easy. In the coming chapters, you'll read about the challenges of ignoring marketing specifically designed to entice you to consume more and the difficulties of making weight loss permanent. You will learn how to balance the need to enjoy festive occasions with friends and family while still controlling your weight. But those challenges aside, it's important to acknowledge that fifty-plus pounds is a lot of weight to lose; as we said, it should take around eighteen months to achieve, possibly longer. It certainly was no quick dash for us, and, along the way, we got frustrated during days when the scale seemed stubbornly fixed, unwilling to budge any lower no matter how disciplined we were. More than anything else, we maintained progress because we never lost sight of the data around us.

Key Behavioral Best Practices
Explained in This Chapter

CORE MICROHABIT
- Be calorie conscious.

ADDITIONAL MICROHABITS
- Don't drink your calories.
- Use a scale to experiment with your diet; keep a food diary if it helps.

DATA

- Limit your consumption of carbohydrates such as bread, pasta, pizza, and sugar.
- Set a realistic long-term weight loss target and smaller short-term targets to keep you motivated.
- Prepare to spend about eighteen months—or more—to lose fifty pounds.

CHAPTER 4

BUYER BEWARE

(Don't Waste Time or Money on the Diet Industrial Complex)

Any dieter faces some pretty strong headwinds in his or her quest to lose weight. We've already covered several of them—the problems of abundance, temptation, hunger, etc. But there's another force at work just as potent and pervasive as any of the others: marketing.

While we fully endorse the free market and the right of consumers to choose what they buy without government getting in the way—even if those choices aren't wise, rational, or healthy—we also understand that this system generally works against those who want to lose weight. Obviously, food manufacturers, vendors, and restaurants make more money if we consume more food, so they are inclined to encourage us to eat as much as possible. We see this at play every time we are offered a "value meal" or combo deal at McDonald's or some other fast-food chain, where, for just a little more money, we can get much more food. We see it when the waitress brings us the dessert menu without our having to ask. We see it in advertisements, food packaging, and, of course, in the rock-bottom prices pinned to some of the most fattening and unhealthy foods available.

The onus, therefore, falls on us as consumers to avoid these enticements. If we want to make better choices, all of us need to stay conscious of the constant pressure from sellers and marketers to get us to eat more. Likewise, we also need to apply the same vigilance when contemplating spending money on fad diets and so-called diet foods designed, packaged, and marketed to take advantage of dieters' overly optimistic desire for a short-term and easy solution to their weight problem. That's why the next core behavioral best practice of the Economists' Diet is pretty straightforward: don't waste time or money on fad diets or diet food.

RESIST THE UPSELLING

If it's so obvious that the food industry is trying to get us to eat more, and that eating more is causing huge health problems, why do we do so little about it? Why does the government and the rest of civil society just watch it all happen from the sidelines?

The answer, in short, is that the free enterprise system has proved immensely successful in providing so many millions of us with a decent standard of living. Free enterprise is recognized as the goose that laid the golden egg, and regardless of what political opponents say about one another, no mainstream politician is about to launch a major attack on the price system and our freedom to choose what we consume for ourselves.

Neither, as some more radical critics suggest, does our freedom to choose necessarily mean we're doomed to end up as dupes beholden to advertising and marketing experts who can bend our wills to the needs of their employers, shareholders, and clients. But being master of your own consumer destiny is easier said than done; that's why we wrote this chapter! We want you, as a buyer of food, to be better equipped to spot marketing ploys that you are best off ignoring.

For the free market to work most effectively over the long term, consumers need to make good choices, meaning we have to take responsibility for ensuring that we buy things in the quantity and of the quality that are suitable for us. Car makers, for instance, would love it if we all purchased a fleet of their newest, most high-tech models every year, but unless you're an ultrarich car enthusiast, you know that you need only a car that is reliable and will last a number of years. The maxim caveat emptor, or "buyer beware," which expresses the idea that the consumer is sovereign in the marketplace—not a puppet whose strings are there to be pulled by marketers—is the economic philosophy underpinning capitalism. Our economy works best when consumers reward good products and services, especially those that are most innovative and useful, while not spending or wasting money on "cheap" marketing ploys that urge us to get better "value" by buying more of a low-quality product.

One of the most ubiquitous examples of this marketing tactic is upselling. You sidle up to the concessions counter at the movie theater or the cashier at your favorite fast-food joint, order a small soda, and are then told that for only a few extra cents, you can get a medium, which contains 50 percent more soda! What a bargain! But is it? Too often, we take the larger serving because it makes good economic sense at the moment of purchase without considering the long-term costs to our health. This was a trap that we, Rob and Chris, used to fall into all the time.

Try Ordering the Kid-Size Portion. Seriously!

A friend of ours recently told us a story about a trip she and her family took to Carvel, an ice-cream store with outlets all over the United States. As she stood in line looking at the different sizes of cones and cups, she realized that most adults would likely never consider ordering one of the two smallest sizes—kids and junior—simply because of their names. But when she compared the calorie counts of those sizes to the small, medium, and large options, she noticed that the kid-size was more than sufficient to satisfy her sweet tooth.

Spotting the smallest size is often made all the more difficult because the person behind the counter may not even offer it to you. For instance, the adults ahead of our friend in the line were offered only small, medium, or large—it never even occurred to them to order the kid-size. The same principle applies to Starbucks: How many customers are even aware that there is such a thing as the "short"?

Seeking out the smallest and most appropriate-sized options takes a few extra seconds of attention, requiring you to turn off eating autopilot. Next time you're out to eat, consider ordering the kid-size portion of whatever you're planning to eat, assuming that one is available. You might feel a little silly at first, but you'll forget any momentary embarrassment the second you step on the scale.

Take the case of Starbucks's white chocolate mocha (with whole milk). A "tall" twelve-ounce cup of this delicious brew will set you back $3.75. Objectively, this is "bad value" compared with the "Venti" twenty-ounce cup, which sells for $4.75; after all, the Venti is being sold for 24 cents per ounce and the tall size for 31 cents per ounce; it's more than 30 percent more expensive ounce per ounce. But look at the calorie content: the tall size has 280 calories versus the Venti's 460! From a longer-term health perspective, it clearly makes sense to put aside any concerns with maximizing value and go for the tall. (Actually, as you'll appreciate by now, we'd recommend skipping the mocha altogether and ordering an Americano or drip coffee, which not only contains far fewer calories but also is much less expensive.)

When you make decisions like these, you have to

remind yourself that the "value" might appear to be in the bigger size, but that on-the-spot calculation ignores the future costs to your health, let alone the cost of buying a new wardrobe of larger clothes. When you balance out the costs and benefits over time, you'll realize that the price of the larger option is much greater than the cash you're handing over right now, making the product a poor value purchase after all.

Chris Says

Just in case you don't believe that there exist people who would order larger-sized value meals because they appear to make "rational" economic sense, I shall offer myself as exhibit number one.

Back before my diet, when McDonald's still offered its supersized value meals, I would, more often than not, say yes to the larger servings. Not only did I salivate at the idea of eating more fries and drinking more Coke, but also I was fully conscious that I was getting more bang for my buck.

And the same thinking was in evidence with regard to the free bread provided at many restaurants. It didn't matter whether I needed or even wanted the bread, woe betide a waiter who forgot to give it to me, thereby depriving me of this seeming bargain.

Look at this another way. Next time you're offered an enticing deal, we want you to stop for a second and consider whether the deal reflects good entrepreneurialism or just a bad attempt to increase sales by getting you to eat more of the same unhealthy stuff. While we have no particular issue with the former, even though it may be fattening, we have no hesitation in refusing the latter. Let us explain.

As usual, there is no better starting point in any discussion of economics than Adam Smith's *The Wealth of Nations*. In particular, Smith's tale of the baker, brewer, and butcher, acting in a free market economy, provides an explanation for why we sell to one another and why, generally speaking, the benefits of selling more accrue to all.

The parable takes place in a small village where the residents decide they want to get ahold of some of the local baker's scrumptious bread. They figure they have two choices: they can go to the baker and plead for the bread in the hope that his benevolence toward his neighbors overpowers his commercial concerns; or they can appeal to the baker's self-interest by figuring out what he might be willing to accept in exchange for some of his loaves.

For instance, one villager, who knows how much the baker enjoys the occasional pint, may elect to use his knowledge of brewing beer to set up a brewery so he can exchange stouts and ales for some sourdough and rye. Another villager, brought up in the art of butchery, may opt to become a professional butcher and exchange some choice cuts of meat for the baker's bread. By appealing to one another's self-interests in this way, the villagers create a bustling economy full of budding little businesses all selling goods and services to one another.

It's a lovely tale with a happy ending: the invisible hand of the free market makes life better and generates more wealth for everyone. And, contrary to common (mis)perceptions, Smith was not proposing that we let greed drive our economy. The father of economics believed that humans are inherently charitable toward one another; that part of what makes us human is our ability to empathize with people other than ourselves. In a small village setting, our baker would likely give bread to those in need. But Smith also realized that the baker needed things he couldn't provide for himself—such as beer and meat—and by exchanging these goods for bread, the brewer and butcher simply made sure that everyone's needs were met. A happy side effect of the innate propensity of humans to exchange was an increase in the total production—and therefore wealth—of the village as a whole.

Smith's tale was an optimistic one about the potential for never-ending growth. Human ingenuity, combined with a propensity to "truck, barter, and exchange" would lead to the increased specialization of work (butcher, baker, brewer, tailor, blacksmith, tanner, and so on), enabling everyone to consume more. The economy needn't be a zero-sum game in which one person could consume more only because another person was consuming less.

Yet while a small town in late-eighteenth-century Britain might well have mirrored Smith's description, industrialization and specialization have over time facilitated a rather different capitalist dynamic. Rather than steady growth, capitalism is by necessity marked by periods of rapid change that can often leave businesses (and livelihoods) in ruin. The Austrian-born American economist Joseph Schumpeter, writing in the early decades of the twentieth century, described capitalism as an economic system that delivers regular "gales of creative destruction." In short, the ability to reap huge rewards incentivizes innovators to create new products, new markets, new production techniques, and new supply chains that, while beneficial for consumers and a vital ingredient of long-term economic growth, also tend to destroy incumbent businesses doing things the old way. It's a more realistic story of change and disruption not found in Adam Smith's famous book.

Think of Apple's smartphone, which transformed the world of cell phones while ultimately leading to the demise of manufacturing giant Nokia, which was no longer able to compete. Or digital photography, which ended up putting one of America's oldest tech companies, Kodak, into bankruptcy.

Creative destruction is also a root cause of our obesity epidemic. The food processing revolution is a perfect example of Schumpeter's description of capitalism. It marked a radical new way of producing, storing and packaging food that enabled greater quantity at lower prices. Food producers unable to follow suit, unless they have niche products that support a different cost structure, face an existential crisis. This abundance or glut of cheap food is, as we explained in the introduction, a root cause of our obesity epidemic.

But entrepreneurial innovation isn't always about big, dramatic changes. Sometimes it's simpler than that. Sometimes creative destruction can come in the form of a burger. Both of us used to be great fans of McDonald's. As you may recall, one of Chris's favorite comfort splurges during his career in banking was the Big Mac meal with cheeseburger for dessert. But ten-plus years later, Chris wouldn't dream of "treating" himself to McDonald's, preferring instead to go to Five Guys or Shake Shack. Traditional burger chains have suffered because the fast-food burger industry is no more immune than any other to the gales of creative destruction.

Rob Says

Before losing the weight, my wife and kids and I would regularly go out to eat with another family that has children of a similar age to ours. Both parents are thin, and as far as I know, they don't struggle with their weight too much. But I did notice them making what I thought were bonkers choices. One time the mother ordered a salad at Chick-fil-A. I was left speechless. Almost insulted! Yet these days I understand and am prone to do the same thing. The occasional treat for the kids doesn't mean you have to indulge too.

All we're really saying is think consciously about what you're putting in your mouth. Don't just order what looks most appealing, unless it's a special occasion such as an anniversary or a birthday. Unless you have made a conscious decision to splurge, order what's compatible with a thin waistline, not, for instance, the 540-calorie spicy deluxe sandwich with 400-calorie Waffle Potato Fries on the side at Chick-fil-A.

It's not rocket science: if you frequently eat out like most Americans, and you always get pizza, burgers, or whatever your personal favorite is, you're going to get bad news on the scale each morning.

Five Guys's particular innovation was enabling customers to construct their own burger: a perfect example of the fragmentation of standardization, allowing consumers to buy products made to their unique specifications. McDonald's, in contrast, with its garden-variety menu available to billions of people all over the world, appears a bit old-fashioned. But also note that while, for Rob and Chris, both Five Guys and Shake Shack have created tastier burgers, the double burger is now de rigueur. These innovative burgers, while delicious, are making it easier to gain weight.

Here we have our quandary: if every step a food entrepreneur took was second-guessed by government, keen to stop the collective expansion of our waistlines, we might not have had the food processing revolution. Nor, possibly, would we have had tastier burgers or vast increases in food choice, as restaurant entrepreneurs sought to bring us innumerable new tastes from around the world. It is because consumers, and not, in the main, regulators, have been asked to take responsibility for their own body size, that we, as consumers, have been able to greatly increase the pleasure and stimulation that comes from eating. We have, to use Adam Smith's immortal words, benefited from the "invisible hand" of the market. Yet at the same time, something needs to give: we can't go on eating more and more, getting fatter and unhealthier year in year out.

So what to do about it? To start, realize that not all sales growth is the same. Acknowledge and reward good innovation with your money. When the food industry offers you something new, it may well be worth throwing caution to the wind and giving it a try. We are glad we gave Five Guys a go even if we have to offset any splurges by a short period of fasting later that day or the following day. (See chapter 6 for more on this.)

However, a more enlightened consumer, heeding the concept of buyer beware, should realize that simply being offered a greater amount of food for slightly less money— like the giant tub of popcorn at the movies, the larger value meal option at McDonald's, or the Venti white chocolate mocha at Starbucks—represents an unimaginative and uninspired way to increase sales. Caveat emptor means that the ball is in your court when it comes to making the right decisions. So please remember that some attempts to sell us more food should be viewed as nothing more than desperate ploys to get us to consume more of the same thing.

BUYER BEWARE

THE MISLEADING LANGUAGE
OF FOOD LABELING AND ADVERTISING

Watch an hour's worth of TV, and you'll learn all kinds of surprising things: athletes drink sugary beverages such as Gatorade and Powerade, slim superstars just love the taste of Pepsi, and America's hipster youth (who are thin; how else would they fit into those skinny jeans?) regularly chow down on Big Macs and Sausage McMuffins. You probably take such things for granted, or maybe you think you're too sophisticated to succumb to such obvious gimmicks. But a quick deconstruction of these all-too-familiar marketing schemes might still help inoculate you against falling for them.

Bear in mind, also, that marketing professionals know what they're doing. The above examples are designed deliberately to appeal to what the Nobel Prize for Economics winner Daniel Kahneman calls our "System 1," or intuitive brain. In Kahneman's own words, the System 1 brain "links a sense of cognitive ease to *illusions of truth*, pleasant feelings, and reduced vigilance; neglects ambiguity and suppresses doubt; and is biased to believe and conform."[1] If we are told that a snack is low fat and therefore is good for us, we tend to believe it without pausing to consider that, while it may contain less fat than its higher-fat cousin, it may still be relatively high in fat and calories. But often, persuaded by our System 1 brain, we fail to notice or care about these things because the low-fat label has grabbed our full attention. On top of all of that, Kahneman tells us that our intuition can be affected by the so-called halo effect: the warm glow we cast on something when it's associated with things we enjoy or admire. For example: "I love Beyoncé. Beyoncé drinks Pepsi. Therefore I'll drink Pepsi."

In order to remain aware of language that may mislead you into eating and drinking stuff that will ultimately work against your weight loss goals, you need to invoke what Kahneman calls your "System 2" brain. While your System 1 brain "operates automatically and quickly with little or no effort and no sense of voluntary control," your System 2 brain "allocates attention to the effortful mental activities that demand it, including complex computations. The operations of System 2 are often associated with the subjective experience of agency, choice, and concentration."[2]

When we say that you need to be vigilant, take personal responsibility, make better choices, and come off autopilot eating, we are saying, in layman's terms, that you need to activate your System 2 brain as often as possible. We already encountered this principle earlier in this chapter when we talked about the supposed value meal; intuitively you are attracted to larger servings because of a relatively smaller increase in price. Instead, we want you to take a step back and properly consider the costs to your health over the long term rather than always opting for today's "bargain."

Okay, now that today's lesson in behavioral economics is out of the way, let's get back to our tales of marketing.

Professional athletes may, in fact, regularly consume Gatorade or its various alternatives (or maybe their consumption ends once they've dumped it on their coach after a winning game), but here's the rub: you are not a professional athlete. If you engage in serious physical training, you might be able to get away with increased caloric intake. But if you work in an office and have a family waiting for you at home, you'll be lucky to make it to the gym at all, let alone exert enough energy to make up for that thirty-two-ounce Glacier Freeze, especially if you're consuming a typical American diet otherwise.

As for Beyoncé, we're just as mesmerized by her as the next person, but it's still probably best to avoid Pepsi, even if it is this pop star's favorite soda pop. The average American (who doesn't have Beyoncé's figure, lest we forget) consumes more than one can of soda each day. It may come as a surprise, but a single twenty-one-ounce "medium" glass of soda contains more sugar than the American Heart Association's daily recommendation![3] We strongly suspect that, in real life, Beyoncé consumes Pepsi (or Coke or any other soft drink) in extreme moderation. In fact, Beyoncé's behavior—as well as the behavior of those Gatorade-hawking athletes and any other celebrity shilling for junk food—reminds us of the old rule that a good drug dealer doesn't use his own product.

We don't think there's anything wrong with an occasional sugary beverage or a trip to your favorite fast-food joint; it just can't be a part of your normal routine. Marketers have done their best to confuse the daylights out of us about what it means to eat healthily. If toned, fresh-faced celebrities can wash down their double cheeseburgers with an icy-cold soda, why can't we? Because it's all a mirage. They can't do it, and neither can you.

As we told you, before we began our weight loss journeys, we used every excuse in the book to explain away our weight problems. Perhaps it was our crappy metabolism or a genetic predisposition toward being fat, but we wholeheartedly believed we weren't eating any differently than thin people do. Part of the reason we felt this way was because marketers had done their jobs. Even as two human beings who like to think our System 2 brains are switched on most of the time, we were confused overeaters.

People who can eat without abandon and not gain weight don't actually exist—at least we don't know of any. This should be self-evident based on the fact that two-thirds of Americans are either overweight or obese, but you wouldn't know it based on the labeling of so many of the products that fill our shopping carts. Indeed, beyond celebrity endorsements, many companies and marketing professionals have developed a subtle message that can easily mislead: no matter how spurious, many packaged foods these days seem to have some type of health claim. The examples are too numerous to count, but representative words include *diet, low fat, heart healthy, fat free, sugar free, low carb, reduced sodium, low cholesterol, gluten free, natural, no added sugar, and no high-fructose corn syrup.*

Rob Says

Prior to losing weight, I was as confused about healthy eating norms as the next American.

I love chips of all varieties: Doritos, Pringles, Ruffles, Cheddar and Sour Cream, and Cape Cod potato chips. As my weight was creeping up, I sensed that my chip habit wasn't that healthy, but I was desperate for ways to satisfy my craving. Rather than cut down, I tried substituting baked potato chips, vegetable chips, and so on—but none of these interventions did anything to halt my continued weight gain.

The marketers had appealed to my System 1 wishful-thinking brain by providing me with alternative chips that I believed I could eat in copious amounts and yet not have it affect my weight. I willingly fell for it.

These days, I still dream about calorie-free Doritos, and I still occasionally enjoy a bag of chips. But now I reach for the kind I enjoy the most—but just once a week!

All such language is disingenuous and deliberately confusing—even that which may be technically accurate. For instance, most potato chips are gluten free. These words appeal to our desire to eat the right kind of food, but they're the words of marketing professionals, not health professionals, and they often don't accurately represent the food they're trying to sell. Yet none of these marketing ploys violates regulations. The US Food and Drug Administration actually provides guidance on the use of certain words—for example, "low cholesterol" can be claimed when a food has 25 percent less cholesterol compared with its "reference food."[4] Yet as our System 1 wishful-thinking brain rushes in, we forget that 25 percent less cholesterol may still equal a lot of cholesterol.

Even though the FDA is tasked with oversight of food and nutritional claims, we're skeptical of many assertions that are presumably being made based on the FDA's rules. Twizzlers boasts on its packaging that its licorice sticks are a "low-fat snack." Sure, but that doesn't make them good for you. If you're a fan of Cheez-Its (and, come on, who isn't?), you might opt for their "reduced-fat" variety without realizing they contain more sodium than the regular version. And do you really think that Frosted Mini-Wheats represent "Healthy Beginnings," as the cereal's box proclaims? Our System 2 brains are very skeptical indeed.

Of course, we're not against the occasional bowl of Frosted Mini-Wheats or glass of Pepsi. We're human, and we enjoy such pleasures on occasion. But we emphasize "on occasion." Marketers have confused us about the frequency with which we can indulge in such foods, and the health benefits of nearly all goods that come in a package are probably overblown. If you need a simple rule of thumb to help keep things straight with regard to processed foods, try this: actual fruits and vegetables are healthy; everything else is probably less so.

Marketing isn't the only way that corporations try to influence the way we eat. In September 2016 the *Journal of the American Medical Association* (*JAMA*) published a study that examined how the sugar industry likely influenced medical findings in the 1960s and 1970s.[5] Apparently, researchers downplayed heart disease risks associated with sugar consumption and instead singled out fat as the likely culprit of coronary heart disease.[6] The *JAMA* report suggests that a group known as the Sugar Research Foundation was able to influence such findings and that connections to the sugar industry were never disclosed.[7] And there are plenty of examples of the same phenomenon in recent times. For instance, the Global Energy Balance Network, a nonprofit research group funded by Coca-Cola, which shut down in 2015, tried to downplay connections between sugary beverages and obesity.[8]

Whether it's a new study or a label on a box, there's good reason to doubt many of the claims made by food companies. We're not going to give you an exact recommendation regarding the acceptable ratio of sugar or fat in your diet, but common sense and a System 2 perspective should go a long way in helping you make the right choices. Eating salads, fruits, and vegetables is probably not going to come back and haunt your waistline down the road. Almost anything else—a soda or donut with plenty of sugar or a couple of slices of bacon with plenty of fat—should probably be consumed in limited quantities.

So how should you cope with all these confusing messages? Here are a few simple rules that can help to mute the effects of food marketing:

1. Cut back eating out to once or twice a week. We also suggest going so far as to look at the menu online earlier in the day and decide what to order in advance.

2. Make a shopping list before you go to the grocery store and buy *only* the items on that list. Also, make sure not to go shopping on an empty stomach! Alternatively, as we discuss in the next section, shop online instead of going to the store.

3. Watch ad-free streaming TV services such as HBO Now and Netflix.

The first two suggestions are easy to understand: they're both aimed at avoiding impulse buying. But remember, even if you're being judicious, you're probably going to eat too much when dining out. Restaurants are good at coaxing us to spend more money, often by appealing, as we've said, to our economic sensibilities: "Would you like to add a side of fries to your order for only two dollars more?" "Appetizers are half priced right now." In our experience, it's easier to avoid restaurants than to consistently try to avoid menu temptations.

Your trips to the supermarket should also be planned around specific meals you intend to prepare. You're less susceptible to the language of marketers when you've already decided what to buy. Hopefully, your grocery list will include lots of fresh fruits and vegetables, and you really want to avoid bringing home junk food. After all, you can't eat what you don't buy. By having the discipline to shop from a list, you're more likely to avoid the impulse to load up your cart with junk.

Our last recommendation requires a little more explanation. How could the type of TV you watch possibly affect your diet? It's really quite simple. Many of the advertisements on television are for junk food. When you watch Netflix, HBO Now, or TV on demand, you avoid those ads. In fact, this could be one of the reasons that childhood obesity rates have recently dipped in the United States.[9] Rob's kids get most of their TV from Netflix and aren't exposed to the barrage of food commercials aimed at young children. As far as Rob is aware, they don't know who Tony the Tiger is—but if they watched commercial TV regularly, they'd probably be begging for Frosted Flakes cereal.

Clearly a blanket ban on commercial TV isn't practical; and, for that matter, lobbying efforts to limit the number of commercials aired during children's programs was rejected by Congress back in 1990.[10] But even if the marketing of junk food on TV became a thing of the past, you'd still encounter plenty of junk food ads online, in magazines, and on billboards. Instead, we urge you to bear this point in mind and make choices, when you can, to avoid watching TV advertisements. Even if you can remain vigilant in this constant assault against your System 2 brain, do you really want ever-present visual reminders of the food you're giving up as part of your diet?

Marketing has its place in society. After all, this book is a form of marketing: we're trying to sell you on our ideas related to weight loss and dieting. Moreover, marketing and advertising play vital roles in informing the general public about new products, which help invigorate our economy. But our general message of austerity, restraint, and refusal is nothing compared with Pepsi's $50 million deal with Beyoncé to promote its products.[11] You may believe you're immune to the effects of advertising and marketing, but there's a reason that companies spend copious amounts of money on this stuff: it works. Be aware of what's happening and try to resist it!

THE INTERNET CAN HELP

Grocery stores are complicit in our obesity epidemic. Yes, you're more likely to eat a healthy, balanced meal when you shop and cook for yourself, but supermarkets, like restaurants, are businesses and therefore are designed to maximize sales. Even if you head off armed with a detailed shopping list, as we recommend, the store is still going to do its best to exploit any proclivity you may have for impulse buying. "Oreos are on sale! Well, in that case . . ." The way that grocery stores arrange and promote their merchandise is yet another example of how sales experts take advantage of our System 1 brains.

In his book *Why We Buy: The Science of Shopping*, marketing guru Paco Underhill estimates that 60 percent to 70 percent of supermarket purchases are unplanned.[12] Subsequent peer-reviewed research led by David R. Bell, a professor at the University of Pennsylvania's Wharton School of Business, determined that impulse buying represents a much lower but still substantial portion of supermarket purchases: about 20 percent, on average.[13] Bell's research also determined that young adults with relatively high incomes—what we (Rob and Chris) were when we gained much of our weight—are nearly 50 percent more likely to engage in impulse buying than a typical consumer.[14] No matter what the exact figure is, we know firsthand that unplanned grocery purchases can quickly derail the best eating intentions. At least for us, impulse purchases tended to include an unhealthy dose of snacks (in Rob's case, invariably, a bulging bag of potato chips), cookies, something fresh from the bakery, and perhaps a six-pack of beer. Rob was particularly prone to picking up unneeded foods that were being offered as samples along the aisles in grocery stores: he was always a sucker for the fresh guacamole on offer at his local Whole Foods Market, and of course he needed a bag of tortilla chips to go along with it.

The entire grocery store checkout process compounds the problem, since it is perfectly designed to get you to fork over a few extra dollars on candy bars, chewing gum, or a twenty-ounce bottle of soda. Of course, this is entirely deliberate and represents an example of what behavioral economists call "choice architecture": a principle that describes how the placement of information or items for sale can have a huge impact on the decisions people make.

Placing treats at the checkout works as a selling tactic because of two characteristics of our System 1 intuitive brain. Intuition, according to Daniel Kahneman, "shows diminishing sensitivity to quantity." In other words, once we've filled up our shopping carts, we don't worry so much about any additional cost or calorie content we toss in at the last minute. We already have $100 worth of food. What's a Snickers bar going to hurt?

Additionally, what Kahneman calls "cognitive load" profoundly influences bad decision making.[15] As we discussed in chapter 1, someone who is overwhelmed by financial worries is more likely to make bad borrowing decisions. Similarly, a person who has imposed eating austerity on himself is more likely to give in to irrational snacking temptations because he's already exerting so much mental effort over his diet in the first place. Often, by the time we get to the checkout line, we are tired, perhaps cranky, and maybe even hungry. We want to pay, get out of the store, and go home as quickly as possible. It's no wonder that, under the duress of this cognitive load, we succumb to the snacks staring us in the face. The unhealthy ones are placed there at exactly the point at which our self-controlled System 2 brain is most likely to have shut down.

BUYER BEWARE

Reflecting a bit, we're almost certain that our unplanned grocery store purchases are composed exclusively of junk food. When's the last time you mindlessly reached for an extra bunch of kale so you could whip up a salad for lunch the next day?

How to Put Together a Shopping List, Especially If It's Online

- Set aside thirty minutes to think about it. Don't rush it.
- Think about the staples first. For instance, each week you may be buying tomatoes, cucumbers, lettuce, olives, carrots, apples, chickpeas/garbanzo beans, oranges, bananas, sweet potatoes, bread, nonfat milk, fish, chicken, minced beef, frozen vegetables, eggs, and low-sugar cereal. Set this up as your standard order so you never have to re-input these items.
- Check your supplies. What other items do you need to stock up on? Olive oil? Canned tomatoes? Whole wheat pasta?
- Think about what else you are going to eat for the coming week. Add some special items to this list if you have a particular recipe in mind.
- Don't look at the chips or the ice-cream section. Remember, if these aren't in your home, you can't eat them.
- Set a time for delivery and place your order.
- Give yourself a pat on the back.

This is where the internet comes in. We believe that online grocery shopping can help curb junk-food purchases—especially ones bought on impulse. Since January 2015, after Rob discovered online food shopping, he has set foot in a supermarket only a handful of times. Prior to that, Rob had been the primary grocery shopper for his family, and because he was someone who was often tempted to overeat before he began his diet, this could result in lots of unplanned and unwise purchases.

Rob uses Instacart for his online grocery shopping, but there are plenty of competitors, including Amazon Fresh, Peapod, and FreshDirect, to name a few. Not only does he save an hour or two each week, but also Rob has noticed himself making healthier purchases, such as more fresh fruits and vegetables and fewer bags of chips, fewer fresh-baked baguettes, and fewer artisanal cheese plates. This is mainly because he does a better job of sticking to his grocery list and making more considered purchases than he would if he were in the store. This should come as no surprise given our discussion of System 1 thinking versus System 2 thinking. In the quiet environment of his home, Rob is able to concentrate on the task at hand using his System 2 brain to minimize poor choices.

Each of Rob's orders includes a regular list of staples: milk, sandwich bread (for his two kids), apples, bananas, spinach and lettuce for salads, and so on. Additionally, Rob and his wife will have a quick conversation about upcoming meals for the week, and he'll add the necessary ingredients to their order. Everything is planned out, which means there isn't nearly as much temptation to pick up a bag of Cheetos or a box of cookies simply because he sees them.

One nice benefit of internet shopping is that you can build your list over time. Notice you're running low on mustard? Add it to next week's list. Notice you're almost out of milk? Not a problem. Rob typically assembles his list over the course of a few days, leaving as little room as possible for System 1 impulsive thinking. One advantage to this approach is that there's no instant gratification associated with the way he shops. Since Rob knows he's not going to receive his groceries for a few hours (at a minimum), he's less tempted to toss something in his virtual shopping cart that he wants to eat right away. He can also easily avoid shopping when he's hungry, and even if he is hungry, there's something far less enticing about a thumbnail picture of a bag of chips than there is about an actual bag of chips sitting in front of you on a crowded shelf. Online shopping can help you to develop the self-discipline that you need to maintain a healthy weight.

Try This Now
Set up an online grocery shopping account and put together your first healthy shopping list.

If you don't have access to an online grocery shopping service, write out your shopping list on a piece of paper. Be sure to stick to it the next time you go shopping.

Psychologists have a lot to say about delayed gratification, and research has linked it to everything from improved academic performance to higher incomes.[16] Delayed gratification is also associated with lower BMIs. In a famous study from the late 1960s/early 1970s, researchers measured self-control in preschoolers by offering them the choice between having one marshmallow right away or having two marshmallows after an unspecified amount of time.[17] In 2013, following this same cohort of people, a team of researchers in the United States found that the preschoolers who'd exhibited a predisposition for self-control or delayed gratification were more likely to be thin as adults. For every minute a child could postpone eating the first marshmallow, it resulted in a 0.2-point reduction in his or her body mass index as an adult.[18]

Interestingly, especially for any parents reading this, the results of this experiment seem to match the anecdotal evidence provided in the book *Bringing Up Bébé*, American journalist Pamela Druckerman's personal narrative of raising her children in Paris. A whole chapter, "Wait!," is dedicated to the French practice of teaching children to be more patient. Druckerman argues that, as a result, French children tend to be more disciplined, healthier eaters than their American counterparts.

While it's not possible to rewind the clock and teach the preschool version of yourself to hold off on gratifying every impulse in the exact moment it happens, online grocery shopping can help you develop the self-control you need to lose weight. We realize it isn't available everywhere (yet), so if it's not an option for you, stick to the alternative of building out meal plans and being faithful to your grocery lists. Of course, this will require some discipline—and likely some practice—but we promise you'll thank us later.

One final piece of advice on this matter: avoid wholesale clubs that sell grocery items in bulk, such as Sam's Club and Costco. This is a shame, because, as parents with young children, we know these stores offer great discounts on bulk diapers and other essentials. But they also offer volume-based discounts on packaged food that you should not be buying. Sure, the party-size bag of potato chips is cheaper at the big-box retailers, but unless you're actually throwing a party, you don't need to be buying party-size *anything* when it comes to food, especially brownies or peanut-butter-filled pretzel nuggets, which Costco sells in a fifty-two-ounce tub (convenient for bingeing!).

We tell you this knowing that, if you're a devoted fan of these discount stores, you're not going to relinquish membership no matter what we say. Chris's wife, Nadia, for instance, has absolutely no intention of ending her love affair with Costco. After a long day at the office, when the rest of us would rather slump in front of the TV, she loves nothing more than hunting the aisles of Costco in search of the next bargain. Even so, she successfully avoids temptation by adhering to her own meta-rule of not buying junk food there—she limits herself to fresh produce and household items, although she'd like nothing better than to buy the five-pound barrel of pretzels.

As we said, if the online option is not available to you—or if you simply refuse to stop going to the store—you'll have to avoid temptation the old-fashioned way. Stay focused on your list and avoid being hungry or tired when you venture out. Make no mistake, grocery shopping when you're on a diet is one of the battles you have to fight in the larger war to lose weight, so make sure you're fully prepared. And if all else fails, perhaps try reciting to yourself over and over: "I will use my System 2 brain; I will use my System 2 brain; I will use my System 2 brain . . ."

DON'T WASTE TIME OR MONEY ON DIET FOOD OR FAD DIETS

Just as businesses market their goods and services in an effort to get us to buy as much as possible, the diet industry also peddles its wares in the hope of getting us to part ways with our money. Lasting weight loss requires being equally alert to misleading marketing claims that are, quite simply, too good to be true. It is as important to heed the advice of "buyer beware" when considering diet food and diet plans as it is when wondering whether you should buy the large value meal, whether you need to drink as many electrolytes as your favorite athlete, or whether it's imperative to grab a candy bar at the grocery store checkout. In fact, some of the most dubious marketing claims in the entire food industry come in the form of diets that promise astounding results, totally uncorrelated with the dismal statistics on diet failure. Our message in the final section of the chapter is simple: don't waste money on diet food or special diet programs.

To maximize sales, a diet plan has to find a way to snare our attention in a competitive marketplace, and one of the most frequently used techniques works against everything we're saying in this book. We've argued, for instance, that one of the biggest contributing factors to our obesity epidemic is the innate tendency for humans to undervalue the future relative to the present. However much we reflect on the costs of bad eating habits in the present, we find it too difficult to balance the pleasure gained from stimulation in the here and now against the dissatisfaction of health problems and related costs tomorrow. This tendency for short-termism is arguably mankind's biggest economic blight. And the same exact problem turns up in many approaches to dieting, from miracle pills to two-week (starvation) programs to more sophisticated dietary plans based on empirical findings, such as the Paleo diet and the Whole30 diet, the latter of which requires adherents to eat certain kinds of foods over a designated 30-day period.

Chris's friend, Jane, a New Yorker who works in fashion, has tried Paleo and was kind enough to share with us some excerpts from her monthlong experiment. This is what one particular Saturday and Sunday looked like:

	Breakfast	Snack 1	Lunch	Snack 2	Dinner
Saturday	Kale and spicy cashew ricotta cheese tortilla	Fruits and coconut yogurt	Veal roast club sandwich	Rooibos tea brewed in coconut, lemongrass, and ginger water	Chicken pot roast with English biscuit
Sunday	Stuffed falafel with spicy legumes and hummus	Apple tart	Chicken in broccoli sauce and sweet potato gratin	Plum and pineapple chia pudding	The antioxidant vegetable yam dish

Our first reaction, was "Wow! That looks delicious." We wouldn't mind eating that over a weekend. But we'd absolutely hate to have to make it, given that many of the items on this menu—like the tortilla and the English biscuit—bear little resemblance to the familiar starchy versions of these foods. The Paleo alternatives to these and many other foods require a host of ingredients—sometimes downright odd—that are not typically found in the average cupboard. Turns out that Jane felt the same way, which is why her food was prepared by an enterprising Paleo chef who had started his own food delivery business. Indeed, she is the first to admit that her own relative affluence had made the experiment possible in the first place. She would never have seen the thirty days out had she not had someone to do the cooking for her. Which, of course, raises another point: if you're using a recipe delivery service such as Blue Apron, then change your default order without delay to the low-calorie option and enjoy!

But most of us are stuck preparing our own meals. So yes, there are a ton of Paleo recipe books, but how many of us are disciplined enough to stay on that diet for the long haul, as well as any other diet that exerts so much control over what we can and cannot eat? Even with someone else doing the cooking, Jane's sojourn into a metaphorical cave lasted only thirty days. And, for that matter, the only couple we know who have experimented with the Whole30 diet—a more intense version of Paleo that bans all grains, legumes, added sugars, dairy products, and alcohol for at least thirty days—made it only as far as day twenty-three. Both of them, who were relatively thin to begin with and were doing the diet as a way to cleanse, reported craving their favorite foods—all of which were temporarily off-limits—far more so than usual, to the point where any benefits they experienced were outweighed by inconvenience and stress.

We firmly believe that the only way to lose weight sustainably is to establish microhabits that don't also require you to limit yourself to a prescribed set of specific foods. The second you start eating only diet food (whether a milk shake or a monthlong meal plan), you are sowing the seeds of failure. To us, there is little difference between paying for a specialist food for a month—only to return to your old eating ways after thirty days—and buying a bunch of brand-new golf or skiing equipment (as per our discussion of "all the gear, no idea" in chapter 2) and leaving it to gather dust in the basement.

If you want to successfully lose weight, you will have to abandon all fad diets, by which we mean any weight loss program that involves losing weight in a short, pre-defined period and/or requires *unsustainable* changes to your eating habits. A regimented meal plan such as Paleo is unsustainable for most people (especially those without a personal chef) and therefore a fad. We are pretty convinced that the damning statistics on diet failure—according to one study that reviewed multiple other studies, only 15 percent of dieters manage to maintain a weight of at least twenty-two pounds below their starting point for three years or more[19]—reflect dieters' preferences for fads and quick-fix dieting techniques.

Equally problematic, if not more so, is diet labeling of certain foods and drinks. Earlier in the chapter, we noted our skepticism of labels such as *diet*, *low fat*, *heart healthy*, *fat free*, *sugar free*, and *low carb*. Here we want to take a more detailed look at some of the top-selling "diet" foods and drinks to demonstrate why focusing on these products is a red herring. In short, we don't recommend eating anything that specifically markets itself as a diet food.

1. *Artificial Sweeteners.* While we applaud food innovation, alternatives to sugar offer subpar taste with contested diet claims. Of course, the logic behind creating artificial sugar is sound: give consumers a guilt-free sweetener that approximates sugar's taste without any of the calories. In the context of soda, this seems like a heaven-sent solution: after all, a regular can of Coke contains 140 calories; Diet Coke no calories at all.

Chris Says

Here's a radical idea: give up sugar in your tea and coffee. I did it, having once upon a time heaped sugar in my tea. It wasn't easy, and I pretty much gave up drinking tea for a month or two because I didn't like it without sugar. But slowly I got used to it and then it became normal. Now when I'm accidentally served tea (or coffee) with sugar in it, I want to spit it out because I find it so disgusting.

I strongly recommend going cold turkey on sugar. You need to change your palate and develop a taste for sugarless tea and coffee. If you substitute sugar for a similar but artificial taste, it can only raise the chances of going back to the real thing.

So who could possibly be against something that seems to solve so neatly the principle we highlighted earlier in the book: "Don't drink your calories"? The answer, unfortunately, seems to be scientists. (Blast them and their clever formulas and experiments!) For instance, a study published in 2015 by Sharon Fowler and her colleagues from the University of Texas Health Science Center at San Antonio found that diet soda consumption is associated with increased weight in older adults.[20] Many scientists and dietitians have theorized that diet sodas contribute to weight gain by affecting the way the body regulates blood sugar.[21]

In other words, artificial sweeteners may do exactly what carbohydrates do: trigger the hormone insulin, thereby signaling to your body the need to store fat. Whatever the case, we recommend staying away. At the very least, we caution strongly against thinking that drinking diet soda will be particularly helpful in your battle to lose weight. We see plenty of thin people drinking regular soda, plenty of fat people drinking diet soda; it doesn't appear to be the determining factor; at least not in the way that exchanging a large white chocolate mocha for an (unsweetened) Americano is! Ideally, avoid all soda except on rare occasions; but if you do succumb to temptation, you may as well drink the version you prefer.

2. *Lite Beer.* This is an issue close to our hearts: we like beer. Our views on this important topic exemplify all that we said about artificial sweeteners, which is not surprising given that lite beer contains fewer calories than non-lite varieties by virtue of the sugar's replacement with artificial sweeteners. Even so, it's worth taking a look at

this particular subset of the artificial sweetener industry because marketers have been so successful in encouraging people to drink lite beer, particularly in America. First some facts, using an average craft pale ale (Chris's favorite) by way of example. A can of lite beer contains roughly 100 calories, about half the calories of a pale ale. But it also contains less alcohol: your average lite beer contains about 4 percent alcohol by volume versus the pale ale's 6 percent.

One way of looking at this—the drinker's perspective—is to argue that a person will go on drinking until he or she reaches the required level of tipsiness. Based on the difference in alcohol content, a consumer drinking pale ale might stop at three pints, whereas the same consumer would "need" an additional pint and a half of the lite beer to experience the same intoxicating effect. Drinking pale ale, he would consume 600 calories; drinking the lite beer, he would consume 450. Both beverages would be calorie heavy, no doubt about it; nor are we dismissing the 150-calorie difference between the two as insignificant. All the same, given that drinking like this is not a nightly event (at least we hope it's not), we don't think it makes all that much difference. We admit it, we're beer snobs, but given the taste (or lack thereof) of lite beer, the switch is just not worth it for us.

Perhaps, though, our argument is unrealistic. Perhaps we wouldn't increase the quantity of lite beer drunk because it contains less alcohol, so both our hypothetical evenings would end after three pints. In this case, the calorie count would be double (600 versus 300 calories) by opting for the pale ale over the lite beer, making the switch to lite beer appear worthwhile. Of course, we should remind you of the research, mentioned above, that puts into question the whole premise behind artificial sweeteners. But the key point is, for the rare(ish) three-pint night, we still don't think it's worth the switch to the tasteless stuff. And if you're out with your pals for happy hour and very focused on your weight but don't like drinking lite beer, then you're probably better off ditching beer altogether and opting for club soda—with vodka or on its own.

To be sure, our own experiments with beer drinking (and we're talking here about a big night out, not a one-off pint) and our scale the following morning are quite clear: it's the combination of beer *and* the snacks, followed by the burger or the pizza that adds the pounds. While we're not recommending you make a regular habit of this, we know from experience that if you can control your urge to eat bad food while drinking, the effect of a few beers on the scale the following day is limited. We're not saying there aren't other negative effects to your health from a three-pint night, but purely from a weight perspective, it is manageable.

3. Low-Fat Yogurt (or Low-Fat Anything). This is the classic example of how marketing can muddle thinking. Chris, for instance, has long-since noticed a close association between the fat content of dairy and his daily weight—

cream is a killer on the scale for him. But when it comes to yogurt, looks can be deceiving. Take, for instance, a standard single-serving container of strawberry-flavored yogurt. Most likely, the full-fat version will contain one and a half times the number of the calories as the nonfat version, say 150 versus 100. There's a difference, sure; but it's hardly a difference that's going to make or break the scale! And both, it should be added, are still laden with sugar. Ideally, you should always buy plain yogurt. (Low-calorie or lite yogurts "solve" this problem by using artificial sweeteners, which, as we've said, may be completely ineffective anyway. Notwithstanding, low-cal yogurts are disgusting.)

Our point is more about consumption generally. Whether you buy the low-fat kind or whole-milk yogurt (which is shockingly difficult to find in many grocery stores), you can't eat the stuff to your heart's content. You have to limit your intake if you're going to lose weight. Therefore, if you're going to eat yogurt, you may as well buy the whole-milk version. This may seem odd given what we said about switching lattes and cappuccinos for Americanos, but the point here and throughout *The Economists' Diet* is about quantity. If you're an addict like us, coffee is a three-times-a-day occurrence—and three lattes equals a lunch's worth of calories! Therefore, you need to switch to a coffee drink low in calories. For us, yogurt is different; we, Rob and Chris, eat it only two to three times a week at most, so it's just not that big a calorie difference to make us switch. And even if we did eat the whole-milk as opposed to the low-fat version every day, the cumulative difference in calorie count over the week would be only 350 fewer.

4. *Veggie Sticks.* Food marketers probably had Rob's dream of guilt-free zero-calorie Doritos in mind when they invented veggie sticks. In case you haven't seen them, veggie sticks are basically potato chips, except that the starches used to make the chips are derived from vegetables other than potatoes. We're impressed by the idea: If potato-based chips make people fat, why not make them out of a different food? But, as has been well documented,[22] the nutritional gain from eating veggie sticks over regular potato chips is overblown. Veggie sticks are better for you than the old-fashioned chips, but that doesn't make them *good* for you in and of themselves. Marketers are playing with us here, utilizing the weakness of our System 1 brains. Veggie sticks may contain 30 percent less fat than potato chips but beware: 30 percent less fat than a lot of fat is still a lot of fat! Don't be fooled by the marketing powers of big numbers.

> **Quick and Easy Fixes for Hunger Pangs You Can't Ignore**
>
> Depending on how you're feeling, try one of the following:
>
> something sweet—an apple or tangerine;
> something salty—a small handful of almonds; or
> something crunchy—chopped-up carrots and cucumbers.

All the above will satisfy any hunger signals you receive and eliminate (or at least reduce) the temptation to munch on cookies or chips.

When it comes to veggie sticks, we would recommend the following approach. Either eat sticks of real vegetables, or, if you are going to eat an unhealthy snack, eat one you actually like! After all, the problem here isn't the potatoes, it's the consumption itself. Our view is that all chips or any other similar variation have to be rationed very carefully. Enjoy them occasionally, but if they become a regular snack, you'll see their impact on the scale, something that Rob, who loves chips of all varieties, has monitored closely. So after starting the Economists' Diet, he trained himself to eat them far less frequently. Instead of being a once-a-day treat, he'll allow himself one regular bag of chips on Friday nights—his family's movie night— or when his family splurges at a Mexican restaurant (no more than once or twice a month nowadays). It's pretty clear from our investigations: thin people limit their chip consumption.

The proof, as they say, is in the pudding. Putting the rich and famous aside, generally speaking, thin people are the way they are without being specialists in weird and wonderful dieting techniques, or adjusting their diet from fad to fad, or filling grocery carts with diet-labeled food. They enjoy the occasional treat and splurge, but most of the time, they eat in moderation and don't waste calories on gimmicks or snacks masquerading as diet food. The same critical (System 2) eye that you cast over the marketing of junk food should also be cast over the diet industrial complex. Anything that whiffs of short-termism and/or marketing should not be the mainstay of your diet, whether it is a short-term experiment with fancy "weight loss" milk shakes, eating like a caveman for a month, or a diet-labeled substitute for your sugar cravings.

Key Behavioral Best Practices
Explained in This Chapter

CORE MICROHABIT
- Don't waste money on fad diets or diet food.

ADDITIONAL MICROHABITS
- Order the smallest size available.
- Be skeptical of food marketing campaigns, especially those using the word *lite*.
- Buy your groceries online when possible or make a shopping list to help curb in-store impulse purchases.
- Avoid volume-based discount stores.
- Forgo sugar and artificial sweeteners in your tea and coffee.

CHAPTER 5

EQUILIBRIUM

(Variety May Be the Spice of Life,
but It's Also Making You Fat)

If you talk to an economist, it won't be long before he or she drops the word *equilibrium* into the conversation. Economists delight in using this term. It's like a membership card or secret handshake that says, "Yes, I know what I'm talking about. You can let me into the club."

But as casually as we may toss around the word, equilibrium is a very tricky concept that can mean different things in different contexts. In this chapter, we use the term in two ways: first, to describe a situation in which, by attaining equilibrium, individuals maximize satisfaction; and second, to describe the underlying state of affairs of an economy. For instance, is the equilibrium state of the economy coincident with 5 percent or 10 percent unemployment? While each definition is different, they both describe a state of balance, like an old-fashioned scale coming to rest with equal weights on both sides.

The concept of equilibrium has proven enormously helpful to us throughout our diet journeys in two particular ways. First, in explaining the basics of how consumers make decisions, it justifies this chapter's central argument that too much variety in our diet can sometimes work against us. Second, we use the idea of equilibrium to explain why keeping weight off is so difficult. Using this knowledge, and while noting that we strongly encourage people to exercise, we make the case that you should not *rely* on exercise to help you lose weight.

THE LAW OF DIMINISHING RETURNS

In general, economists assume that consumers spend money on something as long as it provides them with additional pleasure, and stop spending money on it once it doesn't. And while behavioral economics reminds us that consumers don't always act so rationally, core economic concepts such as maximization, optimization, utility (economic-speak for "satisfaction"), and equilibrium provide effective explanations for our next core behavioral best practice: why, when it comes to food, less variety is often better than more; or, to put it another way, why a repetitive diet is often a better diet. To explain this, we need to take a step back and return to Econ 101 and the basics of consumer decision making.

Modern consumer theory was established back in the 1870s with what came to be known as the "marginal revolution" (an extremely sexy revolution indeed). Prior to this shift in thinking, economists had assumed that the value of any good sold in a competitive market was derived from its cost of production, including the profit returned to the business owner. Our old friend Adam Smith had used this exact reasoning in *The Wealth of Nations* to solve what was known as the water-diamond paradox. Practically speaking, a diamond is much less useful than water, so intuitively, it should be worth less. But according to Smith, diamonds have a high value when exchanged in a market because of the huge effort required to find and prepare them for sale. On the other hand, water, which falls from the sky and which took little or no labor to prepare in Smith's day, has no value in exchange.

This explanation failed to satisfy the revolutionary thinkers of the 1870s, and it shouldn't satisfy you now. After all, water is sold at vastly different prices depending on circumstances—and we're not just talking about fancy mineral water culled from an Alpine spring by fair-haired maidens and served up in posh restaurants for $15 a bottle. In the absence of an alternative, we've all probably handed over $2 or $3 for a bottle of Dasani on a hot summer's day without considering the fact that we can get essentially the same thing at home for free. In fact, we could imagine other circumstances in which $3 would seem exceptionally cheap. If we were walking across a desert and were on the verge of dying from dehydration, we'd probably hand over everything we owned to secure enough water to stay alive. The point is: the value you put on something is related to how much value you personally place on each successive, or marginal, use of it, not the amount of labor put into making it.

The total satisfaction, or utility, that Chris (or any of us) has derived from drinking water during his life is infinite; he wouldn't be here otherwise. But given that he isn't currently wandering lost in a desert, the marginal utility he derived from the last glass of water he drank was probably pretty minimal. As he sits down on his favorite comfy couch after a long day at the office, given the choice between having a glass of water or a bag of Quavers (a British cheese-flavored chip he gets to eat only rarely), he'd definitely opt for the cheesy delights. Because he is fully hydrated, he'd get more satisfaction from, and therefore place more value on, the chips than he would an ice-cold glass of water, no matter how much effort went into producing it.

Paraphrasing *Principles of Economics* (1871) by Carl Menger, one of the economic revolutionaries who first used this concept of marginal utility, it is clear that, in general, satisfying his need for water is decidedly more important to Chris than satisfying his need for Quavers. But when his need for water is already satisfied, the consumption of Quavers acquires the same importance to him as further satisfying his need for water. Chris will therefore try, from this point on, to bring the satisfaction of his need for water into equilibrium with the satisfaction of his need for food.[1] In other words, he won't drink any more water until he's satisfied his appetite for Quavers. After that, he'll try to keep his consumption of water and Quavers in proportion to keep himself equally happy with both.

Most likely, having satisfied his need for both water and Quavers, he'll eat something else in order to bring the satisfaction of consuming that third item up to the level that he has achieved with water and Quavers. If there were ten items available to Chris, he would, in theory, consume each one until the satisfaction he derived from consuming the last unit of each item—their respective marginal utility—was equal.

Of course, in the real world we are dealing with millions of individual preferences, untold numbers of goods and services, and different supply conditions for each product. Economists would say that equilibrium is achieved when consumers divide spending among various products so that equal utility is derived from the last unit of money spent on each, thereby maximizing total utility.[2]

As it happens, a lot of what goes for sophisticated economic modeling today assumes that consumers not only optimize equilibrium in the present, but also that they optimize the allocation of money across time, creating an equilibrium that spans decades. But readers of this book will already know this isn't true. As we've already discussed, half the problem with overeating, as well as our penchant for short-term fad diets, stems from our inability to appropriately value future experiences. If we really sought to optimize spending over time, we would likely forgo the satisfaction of eating that cheeseburger and fries today so we could be satisfied with our health ten, twenty, or thirty years down the road.

But for now, let's stick with decisions made in the present and think a little more about Chris's dilemma with the Quavers and the glass of water. You may or may not have realized that the whole theory of marginal utility and consumer equilibrium hinges on one key concept: the more you have of one thing, the less you enjoy it. Chris loves Quavers, but even he tires of them once he gets to his third or fourth bag. Similarly, having just walked across a desert, Chris would achieve immense satisfaction from gulping down a few glasses of water and quenching his thirst. But after having rehydrated himself fully, he'd become less and less interested in more H_2O.

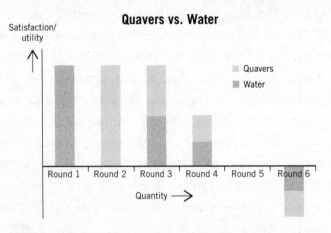

Having returned home from work, Chris initially thinks about satiating his thirst—something that brings him a lot of satisfaction. But then his mind turns to Quavers. He enjoys his first bag as much as the glass of water he's just drunk. From this point on, he makes sure that the additional bags of Quavers are matched with enough water so that the satisfaction from both remains the same. In other words, he's in a state of equilibrium. Still, following the law of diminishing returns, he can have too much of a good thing. By the time Chris gets to round 5, he is ambivalent as to whether to indulge or not—the additional bag of Quavers and water does not add to his total satisfaction. But when round 6 comes along, he is sure. More water and Quavers would be unpleasurable and would actually reduce the total satisfaction gained from his welcome-home treat.

In short, the more we have of something, the less the satisfaction gained from each successive unit (that is, its marginal utility). This is known as the law of diminishing returns, and it is fundamental to economics. Without it, we wouldn't be able to claim that, notwithstanding changes in tastes, higher quantity leads to lower prices. Put in the language of economics, it is assumed that for each product, there is a downward-sloping demand curve, meaning that we (the collective of buyers) expect to pay slightly less for each additional unit purchased. Indeed, the law of diminishing returns and downward-sloping demand curve underpins our whole argument about abundance: specifically, why an increased supply of food, brought about by the food processing revolution, has led to lower prices.

But the law of diminishing returns also tells us that there comes a point when we gain no additional satisfaction from consuming one more unit of something. At a push, Chris can imagine a situation in which he's stuffed himself so full of Quavers that an additional chip actually carries with it a negative marginal utility—meaning that the experience of eating it is actually unpleasant to the point that it reduces the total pleasure he's derived during this particular Quavers eating binge. Intuitively, we all know there comes a point at which we've eaten enough food or become bored with whatever it is we are doing and choose to walk away. This is the point at which its marginal utility has reached zero.

This is where our anti-variety argument comes in. We reckon that if Chris had to live on Quavers and water alone, he would be thin. Because even though Quavers are a deep-fried carbohydrate-based snack, Chris would be unwilling to eat that much of them due to the law of diminishing returns. Eventually he would derive zero—or even a negative—marginal utility from an additional Quaver and would stop consuming them. The very lack of variety would force eating austerity upon him, and as a result, he wouldn't gain weight. It is presumably why there are always stories in the news, like the one we mentioned in chapter 3 concerning schoolteacher John Cisna, about people losing weight after eating exclusively at McDonald's or some other fast-food joint during a six- to twelve-month period. (Chris, by the way, has no intention of giving the water-Quavers diet a go.)

We need to be clear here: we're not saying that a restricted diet can't lead to weight gain. Among poorer elements of society, for instance, a lack of money often leads to diets based on cheap carbohydrates and fried food, causing a high incidence of obesity and related health problems. However, for us, Chris and Rob, as relatively affluent people, the search and resulting satisfaction of our desire for variety was a huge factor in our weight gain. Accepting less variety and, frankly, a little less stimulation from eating has been a necessary corrective in our respective weight loss journeys. In short, expect to eat grilled meat or fish and salad several times a week.

There's No Food in the Fridge, I Can't Get Out, I Need to Order In—but What to Order?

- a shrimp and vegetable Chinese dish
- a delicious curry, one light on sauce, such as a jalfrezi or tandoori *without* rice and naan bread
- a Thai salad
- Thai tom yum goong soup

- Chinese hot and sour soup
- Vietnamese summer rolls
- pho soup

Alternatively, make this meal your one splurge of the week, and mini-fast the following day. (See chapter 6.)

What Should I Keep at Home to Avoid Ordering Takeout?

A Ton of Salad Materials. Put them on your online shopping list now.

Eggs. A hard-boiled egg is a great protein addition to a salad, and a two-egg omelet is an easy-to-make, filling dinner.

Beans. Kidney beans, white or black beans, or garbanzo beans are a base for countless simple meals and dips you can make to keep you from dialing for your favorite pizza takeout. There are, for instance, a ton of recipes for a simple vegetarian chili or salads you can find online right now. We'd recommend looking at food network.com or allrecipes.com or using an app like Pinterest that aggregates ideas from a multiple of blogs.

Canned Tomatoes. Add some fresh or frozen peas and corn, salt, pepper, and cinnamon (optional), and you have all you need to make a great sauce. Throw in a handful of pasta shells, and you have a great dinner.

You'll hear some more recipe ideas later on.

When the two of us were growing up, choices were relatively limited. In England, for instance, back in the 1970s and 1980s, eating out for Chris and his family pretty much meant going to a Chinese or Indian restaurant. Today, with the ubiquity of Thai, Japanese, Korean, and Malay food, just to name some other East Asian options, we have essentially an unlimited number of choices to keep us stimulated. And the choices don't stop once we've entered the restaurant. Given the often huge number of menu options available at any particular eatery, we could dine at our favorite establishments every night without ever really reducing the marginal utility from each successive outing. Remember how Rob and his wife wanted to savor the culinary delights on offer in Boston and Washington, DC? The experience of so much variety coincided directly with Rob's weight gain. Surrounded by less-inspiring dining options, he never would have gained so much weight. Variety may be the spice of life, but this spice might very well be making you fat. One way to reverse the trend of overeating is to commit yourself to a relatively consistent diet. Eating out less is a good place to start. In chapter 4, we exposed the marketing that restaurants use to get you to eat more, and we'll have more to say about eating out in chapter 6.

But the same rule applies to eating in: a bit more boredom will go a long way toward helping you reach your weight loss goals. In the next section, we provide some examples of the meals on offer at Chez Payne and Chez Barnett. The choices may seem rather dull, but that's the point. In fact, you may have already detected an element of sameness in our dietary discussions thus far. Chapter 2, for instance, included repeated talk of salad, cream-free soups, and apples, as well as a sidebar in which Chris extolled the virtues of eating the same cereal every day! We also recommended regular use of leftovers, and while it may be boring eating the same thing again, just think of the time you've saved yourself from not having to prepare an additional meal. In principle, a repetitive diet frees up more time to do other stuff. As for drinks, as we showed in our table on calorie content in chapter 3, we are all about having your one frills-free go-to coffee (for instance, unsweetened Americano) and sticking to it day in and day out. Rather than bemoan your own lack of creativity in the kitchen, revel in the "tedium" of a limited number of easy-to-prepare healthy, and hopefully tasty, dinners.

PREPARE MORE MEALS AT HOME, BUT WHAT SHOULD WE EAT?

We don't know about you, but we often feel a little insecure in the kitchen. Celebrity chefs abound, filling the airwaves with new ideas for delicious-looking dishes. Cooking competitions bring ordinary Joes and Janes into studios only to be judged (or shouted at, if Gordon Ramsay is hosting) on how (un-)original they are. Even though most of us don't aspire to be three-star chefs, the message is clear: eating well means eating a lot of different foods that, ideally, you prepare yourself. Faced with such pressure, it's little wonder that we give up before even trying, placing an order for takeout before we've even managed to boil a pot of water.

It's a vicious cycle of failure that stems from a collective culinary overreach. We don't all need to be a Top Chef or a Barefoot Contessa, however much we enjoy watching those programs. In fact, we can't be. Some are born with the desire and ability to cook brilliantly, and even fewer make a career out of it. Most of us are better off learning some simple cooking techniques and feeding ourselves well enough to get by. If you accept this truth and embrace simplicity and less variety, your health (and sanity) will be better for it.

But let us be clear: you must be prepared to incorporate home cooking into your weight loss plans. If there was ever a perfect example of why this is the case, it comes from Chris's old boss Charles, who dropped weight dramatically over a two-week period by eating nothing but cabbage soup and then proceeded to gain back the weight just as quickly. Both Charles's weight loss and weight gain were hardly a surprise. Presumably, following the law of diminishing returns, Charles lost weight because, after a while, he preferred eating nothing to eating another bowl of cabbage soup. But the weight returned quickly because he'd learned absolutely nothing about how to stop overeating. He developed no new eating habits and had not learned how to prepare satisfying meals at home to address the underlying problem. The strict diet of cabbage soup was, not surprisingly, unsustainable—just another fad doomed to failure.

With all our insistence on home cooking, it is with some trepidation, especially given our all-too-evident kitchen inadequacies, that we are going to share with you the Chris 'n' Rob cookbook. You already know that ours is not a traditional diet book packed full of one-of-a-kind recipes, but people still appreciate guidance on what to eat, and we're happy to provide what we can. "What have you been eating?" was a common question thrown at us by friends and coworkers who were curious about how we lost so much weight. Even Rob's doctor wanted to know! Unfortunately, "Less!" doesn't seem to be an acceptable answer.

Now seems like as good a time as any to share some of our eating habits, precisely because, as you will see, they are generally pretty damn ordinary. Bon appétit!

WHAT ROB EATS

I have a pretty simple rule of thumb when it comes to eating to lose weight: salad, or another veggie-rich equivalent, needs to become the default meal choice. Through my daily weigh-ins, I observed that when I eat mostly fruits and vegetables, I don't have to worry about quantity very much. Put another way: you can eat as much salad or as many apples as you want without gaining weight. The same goes for any other raw vegetable or fresh fruit, but no other food type, I found, has such a minimal impact on the scale as a simple salad. It should be noted, however, that this same point does not apply to many of the things we can put *on* a salad, including dressing, which is often loaded with fat or sugar and can quickly transform a sensible meal into an unhealthy one.

Try This Now

Buy a bag of apples and get in the habit of taking one with you wherever you go (or at least to the office), so that if hunger strikes, you're ready.

Clearly, we don't expect you to eat salad for breakfast (though if you want to, go for it), but I have identified several morning meal options that are consistent with a healthy weight. Before I started my diet, I generally ate a square meal for breakfast: a bagel with cream cheese and perhaps some sausage; a large bowl of sugar-coated cereal; a ham-and-cheese croissant; biscuits and gravy; or a gut-busting breakfast burrito if I was feeling especially gluttonous. All of this might have been washed down with a whole-milk latte or served with a side of hash browns. I could easily consume half of my daily recommended calories before nine in the morning and still be hungry by lunch.

Based on my current habits, while there is some variety

in what I eat, I pretty much stick to this decidedly simpler and much less interesting list:

- two scrambled eggs and one piece of whole wheat toast with Kerrygold Irish butter
- one piece of toast and an apple
- two strips of regular bacon accompanied by a banana-and-milk smoothie (or "moothie," as my daughter, Ramona, called it when she was two years old)
- a small serving of yogurt with fruit; say, a banana or some blueberries
- a small helping of granola cereal with a glass of whole milk

Make Your Own Smoothies

Smoothies aren't for everyone, but they can be a good alternative to fasting or skipping a meal before a big night out. The key is making them yourself at home using fresh fruits and vegetables and no added sugar. You'll need a blender, too.

For a good breakfast smoothie, try blending a cup of spinach, a cup of frozen blueberries, two tablespoons of plain yogurt, and a cup of milk.

For lunch, blend a cup of spinach, a banana, and a cup of coconut water.

Alternatively, try blending one peeled orange, three tablespoons of plain yogurt, and one cup of milk.

But do avoid smoothies you don't make yourself. For

example, one time while waiting for a flight, Rob ordered a smoothie from an airport restaurant, thinking it would be a healthy option. He then watched the employee pour a pink liquid into a blender and mix it with ice. He didn't have a chance to inspect the ingredients, but it was pretty clear upon tasting it that the concoction was full of added sugar and all sorts of preservatives. It also tasted vile. Unless a smoothie is made from fresh ingredients, opt for a salad instead!

For lunch, I made a similar transition. Prior to beginning the Economists' Diet, a typical lunch would have consisted of a sandwich and chips, or a burger and fries, or a burrito and tortilla chips, or some pasta, or a few slices of pizza, or perhaps a sampling of curries from an Indian buffet. I certainly still have these meals on occasion, but they are no longer the norm. These days, a typical lunch might consist of:

- a salad with a piece of fruit
- a half sandwich and a bowl of soup or couscous
- some pasta salad with carrots
- chicken nuggets (baked, not fried) and a side of coleslaw (skip the fries)
- leftovers from the meal prepared the night before

On days when I know I'm going to have a large dinner, I'll often prepare a smoothie for lunch. My favorite lunchtime smoothie involves equal parts spinach, coconut water, and frozen blueberries. Not only does it get me through the afternoon and contain relatively few calories, but it's delicious, too.

Try This Now

Next time it's offered, say no to the free bread, chips, or cookies that come with your lunch order.

In general, it's best to pack your lunch rather than eat out, but I know that's not practical for everyone. It often isn't for me, since I'm usually focused on packing lunches for my kids and getting them out the door rather than thinking about what I'll want for lunch later that day. So when I eat out, I look for places that emphasize salads and fresh ingredients.

When ordering a salad, I always go for the smaller-sized offering (remember: *Resist all upselling*), as I've discovered that's all I actually need to feel satiated. I generally let calorie postings guide my selection; frequently, plain Caesar salads will be the lowest-calorie option (although I occasionally get my Caesars with kale, which has more nutrients than the romaine lettuce traditionally used). At my number one salad spot in DC, Chopt, my favorites are its kale Caesar, which, with dressing, has 290 calories, while its Mexican Caesar, also with dressing, has 410 calories. If croutons come on the salad, that's fine, but I always decline any extra bread offered to me. Usually I go meatless on salads I order, but about once a week, I'll order a salad with meat on it. If I order a preconfigured salad from a menu, I tend to avoid salads with a calorie count over 500. Always be calorie conscious when placing your order!

Lastly, there's dinner, my particular Achilles' heel. Dinner used to be my biggest meal of the day, even though, as you can see, I had already eaten two square ones. Back when I was fat, dinner consisted of a lot of variety and typically involved eating out or ordering takeout. It was something I did with friends and significant others, so there was often a social component involved as well. Most notably, though, I had the bad habit of eating out three to five times a week—and sometimes more than that! What did I eat? You name it. Pizza was a favorite, as was Indian food. I would consume copious amounts of steak, hamburgers, Mexican food, Chinese food, and so on. I rarely held back either, especially at dinner. At a restaurant, if I had the choice between a side salad and fries, I chose fries every single time.

I still occasionally enjoy a meal out (two times per week max), but I try to prepare as many meals at home as possible. More often than not, I end up cooking healthier dishes because I can control exactly what goes into them.

While there's no shortage of culinary influences in my home-cooked dinners, the menu itself is limited and consists of a lot of grilled or boiled stuff. We tend to have meat or fish with our dinner every other night. Here are my family's favorite meals:

- black bean soup made from scratch
- fish tacos
- risotto with olive oil, spinach, and black olives
- fried rice with bok choy or spinach
- pork barbecue cooked in a slow cooker
- grilled chicken with rice or some other grain
- grilled portobello mushrooms
- beef bourguignon

If any of these recipes sounds daunting to you (wasn't Julia Child known for her beef bourguignon?!), trust me: if my wife or I can cook it, so can you. And the internet is full of recipes for these and all other meals at any level of complexity. Your portions are much more likely to be in check when you eat at home, but wherever you're eating, you always have to monitor yourself and avoid the urge to splurge. It is far easier for me to do this at home than in a restaurant.

WHAT CHRIS EATS

The answer, in short, is a lot of salad—no surprise there— but also a lot of grilled meat. Many people have expressed a particular interest in this part of my diet. I am a fairly big meat eater, and it's rare for a day to go by without me eating it. I eat beef, chicken, pork, turkey, lamb, and so on (although less lamb than I would like, as my wife hates the stuff!). Over the years, my daily weigh-in has not led me to view one meat as especially more problematic for my weight than another, and I've been able to combine meat eating with successful weight management. There are, however, two key lessons I've learned from experimenting with my scale: (1) how to cook meat and (2) how much of it I should eat at any one sitting.

In terms of how it is cooked, following on from our theme about keeping food simple, I am a firm believer in eating meat in the plainest form possible: say, a chicken breast, a pork chop, or steak. (More on how I prepare a chicken breast, below). The problem with many meat dishes, as opposed to the plain breast, is that they are often laden with yummy sauces containing cream, sugar, and other weight-gaining elements. Often it's the yumminess of the sauce that entices me for seconds or even thirds! For me, therefore, grilling is the way to go, because I can prepare a plain piece of meat that still tastes great but lacks the calorie-laden sauces. Of course, similar results can be obtained from broiling or baking. (Note: I never prepare fried meat at home.) But by sticking to grilling, I have discovered that a palm-sized portion of meat with salad invariably makes for good news on the scale the following morning.

Chris Says

It would be remiss of me at this point not to mention that my wife, Nadia, is a leading light in the practice of keeping things simple and minimizing variety. Her twenty-year-long weekday routine of oatmeal for breakfast and salad for lunch has enabled her to successfully keep to the weight she's wanted. (As of this writing, Nadia is ten pounds lighter than she was fifteen years ago.)

In particular, she swears by her breakfast of oatmeal. It's easy to make, nutritious, and very economical. Best of all, just as is true of her salad for lunch every day, it takes away the daily agony of choice. If the decision about what to eat is gone, it becomes impossible to eat the wrong thing! It is a deliberate choice to minimize variety.

To save time, Nadia makes a batch of oatmeal in advance by mixing together the following ingredients:

6 cups oatmeal (the old-fashioned variety, with no added sugar and more fiber)
1 cup slivered almonds
1 cup dried cranberries
¼ cup cinnamon

Each day, she scoops ¾ cup of the mixture into a microwavable bowl. She then adds enough water to cover the ingredients and microwaves for two to two and a half minutes. She prefers to use water, as it contains zero calories, but milk is clearly an alternative. On rare occasions, she will add chopped apples or bananas and/or a small spoonful of peanut butter.

In terms of my daily routine, I am a creature of habit. On a typical day, my intake often consists of no more than a small to medium-sized bowl of cereal for breakfast. For what it's worth, I love Kashi Organic Cinnamon Harvest dry cereal and have it most days. (As you may recall, chapter 2 contains advice on how to go about making cereal a help rather than a hindrance to your weight loss regimen.) I have a salad for lunch and grilled meat (chicken, steak, or pork) and salad for dinner. Like Rob, I generally eat my one square meal of the day in the evening, although as you'll note, it's far from a feast.

I know from personal experience that salad can be both delicious and healthy if you know how to make it. Back when I was obese, I had no idea how to make a good salad—but of course that didn't stop me from owning a sophisticated salad spinner! These days, I have no problem with a bit of excess water on my salad (the salad spinner is long gone); what I have learned is that there are two essential parts to making a tasty salad: the ingredients and the dressing. They are the yin and the yang, and one without the other is simply no good. Yet it is amazing how many times I've been presented with a salad consisting of just lettuce and tomato without any dressing. If this is what people conjure up in their minds when they think of salad, small wonder that no one wants to eat it! I'd opt for fries every time too.

Here is a list of all the items that, at some point or

another, I have put in a salad—although not all at the same time!

1. Lettuce, spinach, or other greens, chopped into relatively small pieces.
2. Cherry tomatoes, straight out of a container.
3. Chickpeas or kidney beans, out of a can and drained and rinsed with water.
4. Any type of black or green olive (stuffed or not) straight out of a jar. (For what it's worth, Kalamata olives from Greece are delicious.)
5. Fresh peppers, cut into pieces.
6. Roasted peppers, out of a jar and cut into pieces.
7. Sun-dried tomatoes, out of a jar and cut into pieces.
8. Pickles (preferably not sweet ones), out of a jar and cut into pieces.
9. Artichoke hearts, straight out of a jar or can and cut into pieces.
10. Scallions or red onions, so long as you are unfazed by the effect this may have on your breath, chopped into bite-size pieces.
11. Feta cheese, a one- to one-and-a-half-inch cube, cut into smaller pieces and sprinkled on top.
12. Hard-boiled egg, perhaps cut in two or, if you are taking a container for lunch, just left whole.
13. Corn, either from a can or, better still, cooked on and then cut off of the cob.
14. Pieces of cooked meat. (See below on how to cook meat.)

15. Wheat berries: To cook, put a couple of handfuls into a saucepan, cover with water, and boil. Add water if the mixture becomes too dry. Expect to cook the berries for forty-five minutes, or until they are soft enough to eat. Make enough to last a few days.
16. Cooked quinoa, the seeds of an edible plant related to beets and spinach originating from the Andes region of South America.

Mathematically speaking, there are 8,008 different salads you can create using 6 items from that list of 16—so, indeed, there is room for some variety. Trust an economist to turn a recipe suggestion into a math problem!

I have eaten quite literally hundreds of salads made out of some variety of these items, and my usual salad probably has no more than 6 items in it. For instance, a delicious mix that I can heartedly recommend is romaine lettuce, cherry tomatoes, chickpeas, wheat berries, roasted peppers, and green olives. But it's really all about mixing and matching from the above list. And the great thing about this list is that much of it comes straight out of a container. All you have to do is stock your pantry with the necessary jars and cans and be prepared to do a little rinsing and chopping. Really, once you are up and running, it takes no more than a few minutes to put together a great salad, and, it should go without saying, you'll be saving a ton of money from not having to buy a premade lunch every day.

If I'm preparing a salad to take to work, I add items

until I have filled up the container I'll be taking it in. Then I empty the items into a larger bowl and add salt and pepper, both of which really enhance the flavor of the salad. Next, I add the simplest of dressings: just a little bit of olive oil. That's it. Over the years, and by experimenting with my scale, I have come to realize that cream- or mayonnaise-based dressings wreak havoc on my waistline, and I suggest you give them up for good. You may shudder at the thought of eating this way, having grown accustomed to drowning your salad in so much ranch or blue cheese dressing that it is just about all you taste, but you'll be surprised how a little salt, pepper, and oil—and perhaps a dash of vinegar or lemon juice—can make for a delicious dressing that also allows you to appreciate just how yummy vegetables can be.

Try This Now
Add ten or more of the salad items listed above to your online shopping list.

What you ultimately put in your salad is up to you, but once you have put all of your ingredients together, all you have to do is toss them around the bowl for a few seconds until everything is well mixed and coated in dressing and put it back in your to-go container. Once you start experimenting with this lunch and figuring out the components of your favorite salad, you'll notice that you no longer crave the heavy, carb-laden lunches of yore. More important, by sticking to the salad every day, you won't have to go through the daily ritual of choosing what to buy from the copious options available. Back in the old days, the daily search for lunch always seemed to end up with my opting for a fattening treat. The more varied the options, the more likely I was to make a bad choice weightwise.

Back in my City of London days, I would have been embarrassed to bring a salad for lunch. Lunchtime was for meeting up with friends to discuss—over a hearty meal, of course—our miserable jobs. Now I pretty much always take lunch with me, but this does not mean that I eat lunch only at my desk or never use my lunch break as a time to socialize. It's still important for me to get out of the office and chat with friends and colleagues. In fact, in my experience, lunchtime eateries more often than not turn a blind eye to a member of a larger group bringing in outside food; they seem happy enough so long as everyone else is paying to eat there. And there shouldn't be any problem at all with bringing your salad into a food court with numerous outlets. Of course, another option is for everyone to bring in or buy his or her lunches separately and meet somewhere else—a park, a break room—to eat and shoot the breeze.

For dinner, you should aim to eat more salad or vegetables along with some meat or fish. An obvious option is grilled or baked chicken, which is relatively lean. Take your piece of chicken—most likely a breast—and coat it with a tablespoon or so of vegetable oil. Sprinkle on some salt (I am fairly generous here) and pepper and cook. While I always opt to grill, if you are baking the chicken, put it on a tray in the oven, preheated to 350°F, and cook for somewhere between thirty and forty-five minutes, depending on the size of the chicken piece. You can tell if the chicken is ready to eat by sticking a knife into it and seeing if the liquid that comes out is clear rather than bloody. If so, it's time to dig in.

So there you have it: the complete Economists' Cookbook. These meals may sound dull compared with what you're used to, but that's the point. We didn't lose the weight through fine dining but instead by eating a lot of the same (healthy) stuff. That said, we actually enjoy eating what we make in the kitchen, even if our choices are limited. And we can promise that this habit will help you lose weight and keep it off.

THE PAYNE PRINCIPLE AND THE NEW NORMAL

One of the more sobering messages of this book is that our microhabits can and should be applied just as rigorously to keeping weight off as they are to losing it in the first place. Unfortunately, diets are forever, and not appreciating this point is precisely the reason why so many diets fail. As we showed in chapter 4, the statistics on the long-term success of diet plans tell a sad story.

Successful dieting requires you to move your body from

one equilibrium state to another. Yes, once you hit your target, simply by virtue of not needing to *lose* weight, you will have more opportunities to splurge on your favorite treats. But as much as we hate to be the bearers of bad news, you will never be able to return to your erstwhile eating ways. Compared with how you ate before you lost weight, you will always and forever be on a diet because the amount of energy you need to maintain your equilibrium weight will be significantly less than it was before your diet.

We've done some simple calculations to illustrate and quantify this point. Before Rob dieted, he weighed 250 pounds. As a result, he burned significantly more energy just to do the same tasks during the day as he does now that he weighs 175 pounds. It's not surprising if you think about it: after all, a 250-pound person is almost 1.5 times heavier than a 175-pound person. In fact, according to the Food and Nutrition Board at the Health and Medicine Division of the National Academies of Sciences, Engineering, and Medicine,[3] five-foot-ten, 250-pound Rob, living his sedentary lifestyle, had an equilibrium calorie intake (the amount of calories he could eat without gaining weight) of 3,076 calories a day. The post-diet Rob, still sedentary but now 75 pounds lighter, has an equilibrium calorie intake of 2,533 calories. In other words, bigger Rob could take in 543 more calories each day than smaller Rob without putting on weight.

If you assume that the amount you were eating before you lost weight corresponds to the amount of food you naturally prefer to eat, then keeping the weight off is always going to seem like a diet to you because you will constantly have to eat less than you want to. Going by the Food and Nutrition Board's online calculator, Rob, who lost 29 percent of his body weight, needs to ingest 17 percent fewer calories a day—forever.

Assuming that your calorie intake is proportional to the quantity of food you eat, and expressed as a percentage of your starting weight, we can say, for instance, that if you lose 40 percent of your weight, you will forever need to eat 20 percent less food than you were eating before, just to stay stable.

But in reality, it's probably even trickier than this. As we discussed in chapter 2 when talking about *The Biggest Loser*, as you lose weight, your body automatically slows your metabolism in an effort to get your weight back to where it was. In other words, the 2:1 ratio (40 percent less weight means eating 20 percent less food) is probably not high enough. Unfortunately, we can't tell you what the exact ratio is, as neither of us kept extended food diaries in anticipation of needing to make this calculation. But after much discussion, we have a sense that the ratio we are looking for is much closer to 1:1.

Here is our general rule of thumb: assuming that your calorie intake is proportional to the quantity of food you eat, and that you maintain the same kind of lifestyle as you did before you lost the weight, the ratio of your post-to-pre-diet equilibrium daily calorie intake should be equal to the weight you've lost, expressed as a percentage of your starting weight. If you lose 20 percent of your body weight, you will most likely have to eat 20 percent less food than you did before your diet. If you lose 40 percent of your body weight, you will most likely have to eat 40 percent less food than you did before your diet. And all just to maintain your weight! That is, after all, why we called it the Payne Principle.

Try This Now

Revisit your target weight calculations based on the body mass index formula we explained in chapter 3. Next, work out what percentage of your current weight you will have to lose to reach your target. This same number reflects what percentage of food you will have to cut out of your current diet.

Losing the weight and keeping it off will be tough. But if you start out with the right mind-set, properly informed about the challenge ahead, it's perfectly possible. Indeed, the 1:1 ratio of weight loss to food reduction underscores the point we made in the last chapter about quick-fix fad diets. They fail because dieters haven't learned anything about the long-term adjustments they need to make to their eating habits. That's why, in our view, it's so important to start in the same manner that you plan to continue: learn how to eat less and refuse the temptation to overeat from day one. Remember that it is better to shift from one equilibrium food intake to another at the time of *your* choosing than to wait for your doctor's orders.

Tackling the obesity epidemic and moving yourself to a new equilibrium in which you eat less and better prepare for a healthier future is akin to shifting an economy to a new equilibrium in which individuals spend less and save for a more affluent future, while increasing investment in the real economy, pushing up long-term growth potential. These two transformations are more than just analogues but rather two sides of the same coin; two instances of overconsumption that need to be adjusted permanently in order to bring about a new sustainable equilibrium.

THE ROLE OF EXERCISE

With all this talk of equilibrium, you may have noticed that we've been concentrating all our efforts on the input side of the equation: the energy, or calories, you eat. We've spent little time talking about output: the energy you burn. You may be thinking that rather than suffer the effects of the Payne Principle for the rest of your days, why not just exercise more? Surely exercise might be a way to lower your equilibrium by allowing you to burn some of the calories you eat? In theory, rather than cutting your food intake by 30 percent, with regular exercise perhaps you'd need to cut it by only 15 percent or, better still, nothing at all.

Well, perhaps somewhat counterintuitively, we want to

state very clearly that we do not think dieters should *rely* on exercise alone in their efforts to lose weight. Of course, if you want to exercise, that's great! Go for it. Obviously, physical activity is very beneficial, and you will increase your chances of living longer and probably be happier if you bike, run, swim, lift weights, do yoga, or engage in some equally strenuous physical activity on a regular basis. We recommend it and wish we did more of it ourselves. Ultimately, though, the problem is overconsumption, and that's what you need to focus on if you're going to be a successful dieter.

How do we figure?

Before we get into the meat of our argument, we want to suggest that exercise offers yet another excellent example of the culture of abundance that we talked about in chapter 2. We don't think you should start anything by spending a lot of money on equipment, yet this happens so often. In come the running machines and the exercise bikes that end up gathering dust in the corner until being sold at a knockdown price to a neighbor who will inevitably do the same thing. Likewise, there are all sorts of gadgets you can throw good money at that will track the number of steps you take each day; they're relatively easy to use and may even be accurate, but, regardless, from a weight loss perspective we personally don't see the point. Or, to put it another way, neither of us have felt the need to use such gadgetry in our own weight loss journeys. After all, even if you take twenty thousand steps a day instead of the often-recommended ten thousand, you will not lose weight if your diet is out of control. If the root of the problem is overeating, why bother monitoring the number of steps you are taking? You're far better off focusing on your daily weight.

On a slightly more serious note, our own experience with exercise suggests that it isn't all it's cracked up to be when it comes to weight loss. Chris remembers one occasion when, as an undergraduate who had already put on weight, he was convinced by one of his pals to participate in a game of rugby. Before the game, Chris did a bit of exercise to prepare. When he returned to his dorm, his friend—the same one who had encouraged him to get off his bum in the first place—pointed out that immediately eating a fried egg was probably not the best way to consolidate the benefits of the exercise Chris had just done. True enough, but precisely because he had just exercised, Chris was very hungry.

Skip These Diet and Fitness Trends and Try Our Approach Instead	
Skip This	**Try This**
Thirty minutes on the treadmill.*	Use that time to cook a meal at home.
Doing burpees (a type of exercise regimen currently in vogue) while watching television.	Stop snacking while watching television.

*Of course, exercise is great, but it's unlikely to work as a weight loss strategy.

EQUILIBRIUM

Skip This	Try This
Hypnosis	Weigh yourself every day to break through the tunnel vision associated with hunger that leads to overeating.
Spending thousands of dollars on Freudian psychotherapy.	After you've bought a brand-new wardrobe, save the remaining money for retirement or your kid's college fees.
Ordering gluten-free pizza for a low-carb option.	Skip pizza; order a salad instead.
Going on a ten-day juice cleanse.	Read *The Economists' Diet* and develop new habits to reduce the amount you eat.
Hiding the cookies in a cupboard out of arm's reach.	Don't buy the cookies in the first place.
Creating a motivational playlist on your smartphone.	Weigh yourself every day and watch the pounds come off as a result of eating less.
Committing to never enjoying your favorite food again.	Mini-feast/mini-fast (see chapter 6).
Eating six small meals a day.	Eat three meals a day and make only one of them square.

We can't say it enough: exercise is good for you and you should do it. But exercise alone is not enough. Moreover, and following our experiences, exercise is all too likely going to result in your body craving more food in its efforts to be compensated for all of the calories you've just burned. Before Chris and his wife, Nadia, got married, she convinced him to run a marathon. (That's love for you!) Needless to say, this was after Chris had lost his weight, since there was no way he could have even attempted this feat while fat. Even so, he had to do an awful lot of training, given that he was starting from a very low level of fitness. He did it—and successfully completed the Marine Corps Marathon in Washington, DC, two days after his wedding—but he lost no weight along the way. Not surprisingly, every time he finished a ten-plus-mile run, his body craved and was given food, especially pasta, to replenish its energy reserves.

Rob's experiences with exercise are no different. Even while getting to his highest weight, he regularly visited the gym, but it clearly didn't make any difference. In fact, Rob was a more active gym rat at his heaviest than he has been since losing all the pounds. Before, Rob used to do nearly an hour's worth of intensive cardio (usually running on a treadmill) seven days a week. He's continued using the gym, but he now goes less regularly and typically does only about thirty minutes of cardio. He knows that the weight loss has come from cutting down on what he eats, not from sweating it out on the treadmill.

Joining a gym is so often no more than that classic

post–New Year ritual in which we try to incentivize our-selves to exercise by paying for an expensive member-ship to some facility or another. It doesn't work. In Chris's days of gluttony, he tried it twice, only to visit about three times over the course of two years.

Even so, we're not denying that an extreme exercise regimen will lead to weight loss or help keep the weight off if you somehow manage to mentally conquer the post-exercise urge to eat. Chris's brother Richard lost twenty-five pounds training for a hundred-mile bike ride. But to quote Richard, the best thing about the training was that "I could eat what I liked and still lose weight." Once the race was over, he gained some of the weight back, pre-cisely because he hadn't also trained himself to eat less. Moreover, Richard continues to cycle a lot, but he uses it to maintain rather than lose weight. He likes a good eat-ing splurge (runs in the family), and he knows that he can get away with it if he's cycled thirty-plus miles first. He knows he'll be hungrier after the bike ride, but in many ways, he wants to be hungrier so that he can feast with-out such deleterious effects on the scale. Cunning though this may be, it clearly has nothing to do with weight loss.

But the biggest problem with exercising your way to weight loss, as far as we can see, is that it is just not sus-tainable over the long term. There are many people who get the exercise bug and stick at it for a while. (Chris is not one of them and will never run a marathon again.) But eventually, following again the law of diminishing returns, the interest wanes and the after-work run is replaced by the after-work channel surf or happy hour. As we've found, this problem is only accentuated once you have a family. What with early starts, getting kids ready for school, and then getting them fed and into bed at the end of the day, there's just no time or energy left for a run.

But even if there were time, it is highly unlikely that we would continue our exercise regimen into our fifties or sixties. At some point, even the greatest athletes will stop exercising and will need to eat less to keep the weight off. Just look how many ex-football players or ex-military become obese later in life because they were relying solely on crazy amounts of physical activity to stay slim.

Excepting the rare breed of sixty-year-old-plus marathoners, at some point we are all going to hang up our sneakers. If we rely on exercise to lose or maintain weight, there will come a day when that option is no longer available. Then we'll add pounds because our eating habits never changed. Exercising to lose weight is like putting the cart before the horse. We recommend doing it the right way round: by changing your eating habits first, you will learn to remain thin whether you're exercising or not.

One final important point about exercise: again we'd like to stress that moderate, regular exercise is great for you; we encourage you to do it and, as we said, we wish we did more of it ourselves. But our celebrity, consumerist culture all too often entangles in our minds the concept of exercise and diet with that of bodily perfection. Far too many of us equate changing our lifestyle (losing weight and exercising) with gaining the physiques of our favorite characters from action movies. As we discussed in the context of target setting in chapter 3, starting out with such ideas in mind will set you up for failure. Don't make your resolution one of bodily perfection and perfect eating all the time. Make the changes you need to make in a sustainable way, which requires, first and foremost, cutting down on the overeating.

We want you to move to a new equilibrium that is good enough, not perfect. You need to be realistic and self-aware. Chances are you're not going to exercise forever, and inevitably, as we discuss in chapter 6, you are still going to splurge on food from time to time. You need to take all this into account if you are going to be successful over the long term.

Key Behavioral Best Practices
Explained in This Chapter

CORE MICROHABIT

- Limit variety in your diet.

ADDITIONAL MICROHABITS

- Take a salad or leftovers with you for lunch at work.
- Ignore all quick fixes; be prepared to eat less food forever.
- Focus on preparing more food at home.

CHAPTER 6

BUDGETING

(How to Splurge and Still Lose Weight)

By this point, you may be thinking that it's no wonder economics is known as "the dismal science." Throughout this book, we've offered rather sober solutions to your weight problem: for instance, eat one square meal a day, every day, for the rest of your life. You want to be thin? Then you're going to have to be disciplined and consistent, following our core behavioral best practices like a repentant does the Ten Commandments.

But in this final chapter, we are going to close out *The Economists' Diet* on a more positive note. Because as much as we advocate for self-imposed eating austerity most of the time, we strongly encourage all dieters to splurge—to eat, drink, and be merry—when the occasion calls for it. Feasting is an essential part of the human experience, and there are many reasons why you can't, and shouldn't, avoid it. Any dieter who plans to deny himself or herself this fundamental social experience is either living in fantasyland or committing to a less full (pun intended) and less fulfilling life.

THE ECONOMISTS' DIET

The good news is, feasting won't destroy your diet as long as you practice what we call mini-feasting/mini-fasting. This is our last core behavioral best practice, and it's fairly straightforward: if you feast with your family at Sunday lunch, skip dinner. If you like to engage in all-day rituals of merriment (remember Chris's annual Christmas lunch?), be prepared to impose strict austerity upon yourself the following day (and, most likely, the day after that as well). If a vacation is on the horizon and you want to enjoy it to the fullest, eat less before and after you travel.

THE ECONOMICS OF FEASTING

When Chris married an American, moved to America, and eventually became an American citizen, he adopted the American holiday of Thanksgiving as his own. He learned the history of Thanksgiving from his wife and her family, as well as other important sources (namely, *A Charlie Brown Thanksgiving*). But what he ultimately came to realize only through firsthand experience is that Thanksgiving is, by design, an extreme eating competition, a feast to beat all feasts.

For the sake of illustration, let's take a quick look at some of the standard dishes that get served on Thanksgiving by Chris's extended family:

1. roasted twenty-four-pound turkey
2. mashed sweet potatoes served with marshmallows and pecans

3. corn mixed with butter
4. green bean casserole
5. macaroni and (multiple kinds of) cheese
6. regular mashed potatoes served with sour cream and butter and often crumbled fried bacon
7. homemade cranberry sauce
8. broccoli mixed with Velveeta cheese
9. peas mixed with fried onions
10. stuffing made with butter, fried bread, and turkey drippings
11. cornbread
12. gravy made with butter, turkey drippings, and cream
13. Brussels sprouts fried with butter and bacon

Even for the fifteen or so people that attend the meal, this is still an excessive amount of food. And although Thanksgiving is steeped in a tradition dating back centuries, we find it hard to believe that the meal has always been so indulgent. The modern version can best be described as Thanksgiving on steroids: a meal of collective remembrance refashioned for our age of abundance. One can't imagine such excesses, for instance, during the 1930s Dust Bowl or other periods of economic hardship.

But as unhealthy as the typical Thanksgiving feast is, and as little as it might resemble the original European settlers' version, there is nothing inherently wrong with it—even if you're on a diet. Thanksgiving isn't going to change, nor should it. Like so many equivalently sized feasts around the world, some inspired by religious occasions (Christmas; the Muslim holiday Eid al-Fitr, which ends the holy month of Ramadan; the Hindu festival of lights, Diwali; and so on), and some marking the harvest (Korea's Chuseok; China's Moon Festival; and Sukkot, celebrated by members of the Jewish faith), Thanksgiving is a quintessentially human feast.

The point we need to stress here is that there is no way you are going to get yourself out of feasting. If you are anything like us, you will end up stuffed, uncomfortably bursting at the belt buckle on many occasions throughout the year. It feels like we are helpless to repel the onslaught of the multiple dishes that come our way when visiting friends and family for lunch or dinner. Indeed, all too often, just taking small portions of the copious dishes on offer still leads to a total stuffing. Sure, in a purely rational world, repeatedly turning down offers of seconds would be taken as a sign by your host to make less food, as would recurring experiences of hefty leftovers. But when it comes to feasting, we don't live in a purely rational world.

In the next sections, we'll explain how to go about managing your weight in a world of recurrent feasting, especially given that feasting and its more secularized version—splurging—have become such regular occurrences. However, before doing that, we want to take some time to explain the function these lavish meals play in society, whether marking a special occasion or just as part of the ebb and flow of being hosted by and hosting others. We want you to make your peace with these events and enjoy them. For anyone who's ever watched the sitcom *Everybody Loves Raymond*, we would advise adopting Raymond's father Frank's approach: open the top button of your pants *before* sitting down for a big meal and dive in.

Taking part in ritual feasting is an essential part of building and maintaining one's community and something that you, or anyone, for that matter, cannot do without. In perhaps the most famous work of economic anthropology, *The Gift*, first published in 1925, the French academic Marcel Mauss used a vast body of firsthand accounts of tribal societies around the Pacific Rim to explain such behavior. According to Mauss, the presentation of feasts by one group to another formed part of an archaic form of exchange—what he called the principle of the gift—which presaged our modern commercial society. The gift contained a triple obligation: to give, to receive, and to reciprocate. A failure to take part in traditions and rites associated with the gift was, according to Mauss, tantamount to turning your back on a basic form of morality that impels humans to partake in feasting. It helped bring people together, build communities, and strengthen the social fabric.

Today we continue to give, receive, and reciprocate following the morality of the gift. Ask yourself: Why do we exchange presents at Christmas? Why don't we just each buy ourselves what we want and save ourselves the hassle? Why do we insist on buying rounds of drinks for all of our friends at the pub, when we would spend the same amount of money just paying for our own drinks? We all know that when your friend offers to buy everyone a beer, he's doing so because it's his turn. And yet we still thank him profusely because he was performing his obligation as part of the assembled group. Without the imperative to exchange, often irrationally, our economy wouldn't exist. More specifically, by establishing trust, the obligations to give, receive, and reciprocate help solve the economic problem associated with "the prisoner's dilemma." Let us explain.

The prisoner's dilemma is a classic thought experiment that goes like this: two members of a criminal gang are arrested and imprisoned in solitary confinement, with no means of communicating with each other. The police admit to each prisoner that, while they don't have enough evidence to convict them on the main charge, they do have enough to get each of them locked up for one year. In an attempt to exact a bigger punishment, the police offer each prisoner, separately, the same deal: if he turns state's evidence against the other one (known in game theory as defection), but the other one doesn't do the same, the defector will be set free, while the other guy will get five years in jail. If both defect, then each will get two years behind bars.[1]

From the prisoners' collective perspective, the best outcome is the one in which both of them refuse the deal and each spends one year in jail. However, each prisoner reasons that, *in the absence of trust*, each is better off defecting because if he doesn't, and the other guy does, he will face five years in jail, while the other guy will get off scot-free. Meanwhile, if both of them defect, the most they will get is two years apiece.

The prisoner's dilemma has become a paradigmatic model in economics because it describes situations in which, in the absence of trust, rational behavior can lead to collective suboptimal outcomes. The prisoner's dilemma explains, for instance, why large firms often adopt pricing and quantity strategies that make it impossible for them to maximize profits. It also explains why too little is done to address problems that beset the global economy: the so-called global imbalances between the big exporting and importing nations. Countries such as China, for instance, need their own consumers to buy more of their own country's output rather than rely so heavily on exports for economic growth, while countries like the United States need to do the opposite, exporting more and importing less. With more collaboration—say, on exchange rates and interest rates—this could be achieved to everyone's long-term advantage, but there is little trust between these nations, so nothing gets resolved. Instead, it becomes easier to think in terms of unilateral tariffs and other trade barriers. Oh, if we could only teach the world to sing in perfect harmony, we could have optimal outcomes for everybody!

Naturally, we could go on, but we don't want to veer

too far away from our central theme: feasting. More-over, listing these examples of dilemmas does little to help because we don't have solutions for them. The good news, however, is that, at least on a smaller scale, indi-viduals, families, and other groups successfully estab-lish trust all the time by breaking bread together and demonstrating their generosity and hospitality. By low-ering the chances of future defection, communal feasting solves myriad small-scale prisoner-style dilemmas. Trust is established precisely because the giver is seen to be overly generous and the receiver willing to accept sec-onds, let alone dessert.

While the obligations of gift giving, receiving, and reciprocating described by Marcel Mauss feel out of place in much of our commercial world, the morality of the gift does explain how interacting groups of people create the necessary trust to provide better outcomes for all, even extending to relations between countries. Ask yourself why diplomatic visits require everyone to attend giant, extravagant, multicourse dinners where the host nation attempts to overwhelm the visiting officials and VIPs with incredible and ostentatious acts of generosity. Of course, guests are obliged to eat whatever is placed in front of them for fear of offending their host.

We don't believe it's an exaggeration to say that feast-ing lies at the very core of celebrations and holidays that facilitate trust, the bedrock of family and community. What is the common theme underlying social gatherings such as weddings, birthdays, Christmas, and Thanksgiving? Answer: food, served in multiple courses that include luxuriant sweets and cakes. Quite literally, the host is required to spoil us, often spending far more than he or she should in the process. In turn, guests are obliged to receive and indulge to excess. To not show up or refuse to eat would be considered rude, perhaps insulting, and could even result in weakening the bonds holding host and guest together. And even if your host is your favorite aunt who will invite you back another time regardless, you can rest assured she will have derived less joy from serving you because you did not uphold your end of the bargain. And no one wants to make their favorite aunt unhappy.

Trust and community are established by receiving food graciously, overeating, and, at some point in the future, reciprocating the gesture by putting on a similarly lavish event. While all cultures are different, some requiring more overwhelming generosity than others, we all share the desire to honor our guests and, as a result, prepare too much food.

If your families and friends are anything like ours, and we suspect they are, just remember what we've said the next time you pay them a visit for Sunday lunch. When presented with such abundance at the dinner table, don't hold back. Perform your obligation to eat too much, accept hospitality, and be merry.

SHORT-TERM TACTICS, LONG-TERM STRATEGY

So how do we cope with the feast when Christmas, Thanksgiving, birthdays, and other special occasions come around, knowing full well that by indulging, we are going to put on a couple of pounds? Our solutions can, roughly speaking, be divided into the tactical and the strategic. By tactical, we mean what you can do to combat overeating on the occasion itself; while we take a more long-term perspective when thinking strategically. Let's start with the tactical.

No one in the world is better at tactical undereating than Chris's mother-in-law, Khawla. As an Arab American who grew up in Jordan, she is the product of a culture that exalts the honorific feast. If you have ever been invited to dinner by an Arab friend, you know what we're talking about. In this culture, overpreparing food is taken to unimaginable heights. And as much as it's problematic for our waistlines, it's wonderful to be on the receiving end of such hospitality and generosity. (For the record, we have spoken to many people from many different backgrounds and cultures who report exactly the same treatment from their mothers and mothers-in-law.)

It should be pointed out first and foremost that Khawla likes to host. Though it causes some mild irritation to her four daughters, it's clear that she prefers the obligation to give liberally rather than the obligation to receive. And, as a host, she has developed a keen ability to enjoy vicarious eating, claiming that she derives more pleasure from seeing her loved ones enjoy the food she has prepared than she does from eating it herself. Even so, she's keen to taste what she's cooked, and invariably pressure is placed on her to eat something. As a result, Khawla has developed some meta-rules to keep herself from overeating at family feasts:

- Eat as little bread, rice and pasta as possible.
- Eat only "real" chocolate with high cocoa content. (Khawla claims that milk chocolate, whether in candy or a cake, is a poor substitute for the darker stuff and has more calories to boot, as the cocoa content in milk chocolate is diluted with sugar and cream.)
- Don't eat fried food. (Khawla conjures up an unpleasant image of oil floating around her stomach to help her stick to this rule.)
- Harness the law of diminishing returns to convince yourself that you can gain all the pleasure you need from a delicious dish by savoring just one or two bites.
- Eat slowly.
- Use mantras, such as Khawla's favorite—"I am not a garbage disposal"—to enhance willpower to stop eating food just because it is placed in front of you.

Chris's mother-in-law is living proof that it is possible to turn rules of thumb into unbreakable habits that successfully self-impose eating austerity. All the same, it's not easy, especially if, like Rob and Chris, you've spent multiple years, perhaps a decade or more, developing the habit of splurging on good food whenever it's available. We are expert overeaters on special occasions. As such, the only tactical suggestion that Chris has developed when at his mother-in-law's feasts, which are generally presented as a buffet, is to try to eat last and, at all costs, avoid eating first. Chris has noticed that if you go first, there is far more time to indulge in second (and third) helpings before dessert is brought out, so eating last will likely mean you have less time to consume additional food.

For the two of us, and we suspect for you, there is little hope of avoiding feasting completely. Instead, we suggest a more strategic or longer-term approach that consists of mini-feasting/mini-fasting. The rule is simple: enjoy the splurge, but be prepared to skip a meal afterward. If the feast was excessive—for example, Thanksgiving lunch—you may need to avoid eating for the next twenty-four hours. This, our final core microhabit, has proven critical to maintaining our weight loss over the years.

Mini-feasting/mini-fasting is, of course, just another way to self-impose eating austerity, pretending that food is scarcer than it actually is. It is, in fact, a form of budgeting that humans have practiced throughout time, enabling reconciliation between the desire to eat large meals and the lack of monetary means (or food) to enable such eating habits. Specifically, by dint of scarcity, humans have learned how to eat less most of the time so as to be able to enjoy eating more on rarer occasions. We saw this, for instance, when describing the eating habits of early American colonialists in chapter 2; such practices also enable the extravagant feasting described by Marcel Mauss in *The Gift*. And it goes on today: in many populous but poor countries, one meal is necessarily skipped each day in order to ensure that the other two meals of the day are larger in size.[2]

Rather than being forced into this kind of budgeting by our material circumstances, in the age of abundance, we need to invoke our innate budgeting skills to enable us to take in fewer calories most of the time so that we can enjoy opportunities for feasting and splurging. Mini-feasting/mini-fasting, as a form of budgeting, has to be self-imposed and practiced regularly. What we are saying may sound daunting, but we promise it's not anywhere near as bad as it sounds.

Budgeting with money, for instance, is something we do to a lesser or greater extent all the time, so there's no reason those same skills can't be applied to budgeting your food intake. Although it's true that some people live well beyond their means, while many others are not good at saving for the future, most people are able, over the course of a year, to match their spending and their income. How? By understanding that there is a limit to what can be spent and paying a basic amount of attention to that limit. Children learn this habit from the moment they get pocket money; through experience, they soon work out how to spend their $5 to $10 allowance over the week without blowing it all in the first few minutes. Some kids even manage to save up over a period of time for a larger purchase.

The vast majority of households with, say, a $75,000 annual income, know full well they can't adopt a $150,000 lifestyle. To afford what they need and want, they know that certain expenses, such as the annual family vacation, require sacrifices—by which we mean forgoing other consumption. This loss of consumer utility may take place before the vacation, as the family saves up in advance, or it may take place afterward, as money is channeled toward paying off the credit card bill racked up during their week in Hawaii rather than being spent elsewhere. Either way, using money for a vacation means, by definition, not having it available to spend on something else at another time.

In fact, the most commonly heard pieces of advice given to people trying to budget and manage their finances falls into three broad areas:

1. Be realistic about what can be achieved.
2. Make a clear separation of needs from wants.
3. Look ahead and anticipate expenses over a whole year or more.

BUDGETING

We could hardly imagine advice more pertinent to dieting. Be realistic: as we said in chapter 5, don't set yourself up for failure by demanding the perfect physique. Separate needs from wants: you may always want large meals, but as we said in chapter 2, you need only one square meal a day, with two other lighter meals.

Finally, look ahead and anticipate: this implies "saving up" in advance of a large meal or a feasting-heavy vacation that is firmly marked in your calendar. Alternatively, skip a meal after a feast, or self-impose eating austerity for a couple of weeks after the vacation, in order to pay off those calorie debts. Indeed, it is precisely because some expenses (such as repairs to your car) or feasts (a great night out with colleagues that begin spontaneously as "innocent" happy hour drinks, only to descend into the full works with a large meal) are unexpected that we so often find ourselves balancing the books after the event. This is all part and parcel of the mini-feasting/mini-fasting lifestyle that reflects the realities of normal day-to-day life.

CYCLES OF BOOM AND BUST

We developed our mini-feasting/mini-fasting behavioral best practice because we realized that any attempt to renounce feasting altogether is futile, particularly when we are marking a special occasion or celebration. When such events occur, rather than holding back, we need to enjoy the moment, knowing, of course, that we will need to offset it with a mini-fast over the following days.

We admit, however, that there is an important caveat to this particular practice. Up to this point, we've been talking about feasts as if they are relatively rare occurrences, but we recognize that in our age of abundance, we can use pretty much any reason as an excuse to splurge. While we may not indulge in a twelve-course Thanksgiving dinner any day of the week, we certainly have marked less sacred occasions with large meals. Your friend got a promotion? Drinks and dinner at the pub after work! Your daughter got straight As on her report card? A pizza party to celebrate! It's Friday, and you had a rough week? Let's ring in the weekend by going to our favorite restaurant for dinner! So rampant has our splurging become that the value we as human beings have traditionally attached to feasts has been undermined by their all-too-regular occurrence.

At the beginning of the book, Rob explained that one of the reasons he got fat was because he had wanted to sample all the different restaurants on offer to him. Some weeks he was eating out or ordering takeout dinners as much as five times, if not more, as if he were celebrating his good fortunes with a nightly feast. No wonder he gained so much weight! Yet while it is absolutely essential to cut down the number of restaurant visits you make each week (see the next section), we know from personal experience that cutting out these outings entirely is practically impossible to do.

Over the long term, lasting weight loss will come from eating less. And while the average day will consist of one square meal and two smaller meals, there will be times during which it will feel like you are lunging from extreme to extreme, boom to bust, with repeated bouts of mini-feasting and mini-fasting.

To be clear, we are not suggesting you starve yourself or go on a monthlong hunger strike to make up for over-consumption. By mini-fasting, we really do mean just skipping a meal to make room for a large meal that you either just had or are planning to have. Are you going out to dinner with a group of friends? Skip lunch. Did a loved one make you a huge breakfast or brunch that you simply couldn't refuse? Skip lunch or dinner later that day.

Nor are we suggesting that skipping a meal is easy; it runs, as we have discussed, afoul of our current cultural norms. But we also don't think the idea is so far-fetched. For example, the world's mainstream religions regularly require their followers to skip meals (though the purpose of such fasting isn't to lose weight). Muslims fast during the day for the entire month of Ramadan. Jews fast for a twenty-five-hour period on Yom Kippur, their holiest day of the year. And Christians regularly commit to ritual fasting during the season of Lent, often by giving up certain foods that are considered guilty pleasures, such as candy or dessert. But before they commence this six-week period of abstinence, they let loose with a no-holds-barred party known as Fat Tuesday, or

Mardi Gras. Our thoughts on fasting mirror this same concept: occasional gluttony tempered by purposeful restraint.

We come at this from experience. We have regularly observed the benefits of fasting in our own lives. We know that fasting has a profound effect on our daily weigh-in, and we also know that you'll get better at it the more you do it.

It won't be easy at first, so having a supportive group of people around you will definitely help. For example, Rob regularly gets invited to upscale steak houses such as Bobby Van's or the Capital Grille to discuss his research with customers and prospects. In truth, Rob doesn't get a huge kick from going to these kinds of restaurants, but they're surprisingly hard to avoid—and most important, portion control is almost impossible to manage in these settings. As anyone who has ever participated in a big business lunch will recognize, when everyone else is eating steak and fries, the peer pressure to conform is very difficult to overcome. So in order to make room for big meals, Rob often skips dinner on days when he has a "fat business lunch."

Tips for Avoiding Overeating at Business Lunches, Dinners, and Receptions

- Check out the restaurant menu on the internet and commit to a good, healthy choice beforehand.

BUDGETING

- Commit to always having the same healthy dish, be it fish or grilled chicken or a salad. Take choice out of the equation.
- Avoid having dessert. If you're with a client who wants one, have a coffee instead. If you feel compelled to order dessert, always opt for sorbet if it's on offer, as it is fat free. Better still, if it's available, order fruit. If you're the client, don't have dessert.
- If there is a catered event in the office, make sure the person doing the ordering includes an order of fruit for you for dessert.
- If you're at a buffet, don't stand near it; mingle and work the room instead. Likewise, if you're eating at a buffet restaurant, don't sit near the buffet; there's no need to constantly remind yourself of all the different foods you could be sampling.
- If canapés are passing around the room and, like us, you simply can't resist, then accept that by the time you are done, these delicious morsels will have added up to your square meal of the day, if not a splurge.

Luckily, Rob is fortunate to have an understanding wife. At least once a week, he comes home from work and announces, "I ate too much at lunch, so I'm skipping dinner tonight." On days when his wife has prepared a meal, this doesn't always sit well with her, but she appreciates all of the weight he's lost, so she tries to be supportive.

Of course, over time, Rob has managed to do a better job of looking at his diary and giving advance notice about whether he'll be eating dinner or not.

Even when Rob is mini-fasting, he makes an effort to sit at the table with his wife and children while they eat so he can still participate in this important family time. It takes a lot of mental discipline to abstain while the people around you are eating, so if you find yourself in a similar situation, it might be useful to explore a concept we call "near-fasting." This is an alternative to complete abstention that allows you to replace a full meal with something comparatively innocuous, like an apple, which has so few calories that it won't affect your daily calorie intake in any significant way.

Mini-feasting/mini-fasting also works when anticipating a large evening meal, such as an outing with friends after work or a date with your wife. When you know you're going to eat a lot at dinner, you will do a lot less damage on the scale the next morning if you can motivate yourself to skip or near-fast for lunch.

We can both attest to this. Like many friendships, ours grew out of a shared work experience interspersed with regular trips to the bar after work. Generally, we just grabbed a few beers, but on the rare occasion when food was involved, we'd boast about how we'd skipped lunch, or maybe even breakfast and lunch, in preparation for the night out. Skipping a meal became a badge of honor for us, and we would proudly report our successes to each other. Mini-fasting had become the price of an evening out on the town, and whenever we tucked into a burger and fries or any other calorie-filled concoction, we felt like we'd earned it. Having a friend to bond with over these experiences not only holds you accountable but also makes mini-fasting a little easier because you know you're not going it alone.

Although most of these shared splurges occurred in the evening (when we could have an extra beer or two and not have to worry about going back to the office), we generally recommend that you avoid large dinners. Perhaps it's because we weigh ourselves first thing every morning, but we have found that eating a big meal late at night seems to really pack on the pounds. Culturally speaking, this may be difficult to manage, since dinner is frequently the most social meal of the day. Even so, we strongly recommend that when you do splurge with family or friends (for us, splurging alone is an absolute no-no), whether at home or in a restaurant, make it a weekend treat and do it at lunch instead of dinner. On this point, let's not forget brunch, a concept that was invented as much for the social aspect (and the excuse to drink copious amounts of mimosas and Bloody Marys in the midafternoon) as it was for the food.

We're not the first to offer such guidance. Ages ago, nutritionist and author Adelle Davis coined the memorable phrase "Eat breakfast like a king, lunch like a prince, and dinner like a pauper." Intuitively, this seems to make sense: if you eat a big meal late at night, your body isn't going to have much time to process the food before you go to bed.

We should note, however, that this classic formulation runs counter to US government guidance on the subject. For instance, the US Department of Agriculture's Weight Control Information Network has been widely quoted as saying: "It does not matter what time of day you eat. It is what and how much you eat and how much physical activity you do during the whole day that determines whether you gain, lose, or maintain your weight. No matter when you eat, your body will store extra calories as fat."[3] That said, there have been a number of controlled studies on this topic conducted recently, and, it's fair to say, the jury is still out.

In our experience, we have found it very helpful to avoid large meals at night. You could chalk our views up to a variety of behavioral factors. Maybe we're likely to consume more calories at an evening meal than a daytime meal, or maybe we're less likely to make healthy choices in the evening due to tiredness, or perhaps alcohol is more likely to be involved at evening meals, thus lowering our inhibitions about quantity and quality. But the most convincing explanation we've found comes from monitoring our own behavior. Put simply, when we splurge at lunch, we have more time in the rest of the day to eat less. For us, it seems to be easier to control our eating once we have filled ourselves up at lunch than it does to control our eating during the day in advance of a preplanned large evening meal. Put in the language of budgeting, we find it easier to pay off our eating debts after the fact than it is to save up spare capacity in advance.

BUDGETING

We suspect that some of you still believe that fasting or near-fasting is rather extreme. Perhaps you're thinking that you don't need to skip meals to successfully control your weight. We concede that this may be the case for some (lucky) people, but if you're obese, as we both were, fasting is something you're definitely going to have to do so long as you want to make room for an occasional pizza, burger, or other food binge.

In fact, somewhat counterintuitively, now that our BMIs are in the normal range, we practice mini-feasting/mini-fasting even more. To some extent, this reflects the fact that, even though diets are forever, because we don't have to *lose* weight, we can splurge more often and quickly offset the effects on the scale by skipping a meal. Remember, we're not trying to be the Sexiest Men Alive, so as long as we maintain our current weight, we're happy.

However, and perhaps more to the point, our lives generally follow a pattern in which we tend to feast on the weekend—sometimes for a special occasion, sometimes not—and eat relatively lightly during the week. This doesn't mean that we never have to mini-fast on the weekend. (After a recent Saturday lunchtime trip to Five Guys, for instance, Chris ate nothing for the rest of the day and still woke up on Sunday morning weighing an extra pound and a half.) But it does mean that these weeklong cycles of booms and busts allow us to enjoy the good times with our friends and families without gaining weight over the long haul. Sure, we might be up two or three pounds come Monday morning, but, in these cases, we will set ourselves a target of losing the weight over the course of the week and set out to eat sensibly over the next few days.

Does this habit make us strange? We don't think so. In fact, in describing this pattern of weekend gluttony followed by weekday restraint, we are illustrating one of the core themes of this book: that thin people behave differently. As a matter of fact, if you query your thin friends, you're likely to hear them describe similar eating habits. When we explained this concept to one of our thin friends, she remarked, "I thought that's what everyone did!"

HOW MANY SPLURGES A WEEK?

As our brief description of religious rituals showed, we aren't the first people to tout the benefits of fasting. Many scientific studies also attest to the advantages, both for weight loss and overall health. The effects of fasting and caloric restriction have been studied mostly in small animals. (After all, it's not exactly easy to find a group of humans who will agree to fasting bouts throughout their entire lives while allowing scientists to observe the results.) Quite astoundingly, among rats and similar animals that have relatively short life-spans, cutting calories by one-third through intermittent fasting has been shown to extend the animal's life-span by roughly a third.[4]

Scientists aren't exactly sure why this is the case. One

possible explanation is that animals that fast exhibit lower metabolic rates, which may explain why they live longer than their comparatively well-fed peers. When metabolism slows, cells don't need to divide or replicate as frequently to make up for damage caused by the body's metabolic processes. The slower your cells die, the longer you live.[5] Also it should be noted that fasting animals are thinner and healthier overall, showcasing decreased body fat, lower rates of heart disease, and improved insulin sensitivity.[6]

Similar experiments have been conducted with primates. A study published in 2014 in the journal *Nature* found that reducing calories by about 30 percent below normal in rhesus monkeys increased their life-spans significantly.[7] In addition to living longer, the monkeys had lower body fat, better muscle tone, and less hair loss.[8]

While it must be borne in mind that the results of animal studies are often not reproducible in people, the bottom line is that from a general health perspective, there appear to be benefits from fasting that exceed weight loss. That said, while we, Rob and Chris, have already explained the important role fasting has played in our own weight loss journeys, it will hopefully be a very long time before we have much to say about the impact it's had on our longevity. And, of course, we'll never know how long we would have lived had we not practiced mini-fasting.

All the same, you may still be left asking, "How many splurges can I get away with each week?" We wish we could provide a definitive answer to this question, but we can't, because, in truth, all splurges are different.

At this point, it's important to remember the distinction between a square meal and a splurge, because your response to each is going to be very different. In chapter 2, we defined a splurge as a meal that contains at least half of your daily calorie intake, assuming neither weight gain nor weight loss: a burger, fries, and a couple of beers qualifies as a splurge.

You can eat one square meal a day so long as the other two meals are light and feel confident that you'll be able to control your weight. If you are currently obese, then the move to this regimen will be reflected on the scale immediately. If we employ the logic of the Payne Principle, the same eating patterns will enable you to maintain your lower weight, having reached your target. Conversely, if you splurge, then, at best, you can expect to maintain your weight on any one day by skipping another meal entirely. In fact, when we, Rob and Chris, really go for it, we often find that skipping one meal is not enough to offset a splurge's effect on the scale the next morning. Getting back to our target weight after Thanksgiving, for instance, invariably takes a couple of austere days, even if on the day itself, we had no breakfast or dinner.

At this point, it is worth repeating another comment we made back in chapter 2: *as long as you're permanently relying on someone else to tell you what represents overeating and what doesn't, you'll never truly have your weight under control.* Likewise, a thorough knowledge of what constitutes a square meal and what constitutes a splurge is going to come from your daily experimentation with your scale. The good news is that it won't take long before you have a clear understanding of those meals that require a mini-fast and those that don't.

Clearly, you need to be careful with restaurant outings, as many of these trips can slip into splurge territory, requiring some degree of significant budgeting before or after the event. This is not surprising, as almost every economic incentive is stacked against you when you dine out. Succeeding in the restaurant business is notoriously difficult, so in order to make money, restaurants focus menus on low-cost (often carbohydrate-laden) foods that appeal to our sense of value. Along these lines, restaurateurs are heavily incentivized to make desserts as enticing as possible, since the sugar and flour used to make them are cheaper to procure than more perishable or complex items such as meat, fish, and vegetables. On top of all this, as we explained in chapter 4, restaurants have proved very adept at selling us more food by exploiting our economically rational search for the best value for money.

Based on our experience, we've concluded that around half of our splurges can be offset by skipping a meal, while the other half—Chris's trip to Five Guys, for instance—take a day or two to counteract. The upshot of all this is that without due care and attention being paid to the scale, persistent mini-feasting/mini-fasting will make weight loss challenging. After all, if a splurge takes two days to counteract on the scale, multiple splurges per week will, on average, leave your body little time in between to drop a pound or two. Because we, Rob and Chris, are focused on maintaining our weight, we can get away with two splurges a week, with appropriate mini-fasting and additional austerity eating if the splurges require it. A dieter in weight loss mode, however, can probably afford to let go only once a week. And even then, he or she will need to be careful to ensure that the splurge is limited enough to be offset by skipping one meal without its effects rolling into the following day.

How to Keep a Burger Outing Under Control

- Remove some of the bread inside the bun. It's a bit messy but a good idea if the bun is particularly large.
- Always ask for a burger without mayonnaise or the house special sauce. Add tomato ketchup later on.
- If you must have fries, eat them only when they're piping hot and therefore at their most tasty. Once they cool, they're much less enjoyable and easier to push aside.
- Always ask for a single burger rather than take the double-burger option.
- If you're eating a burger at a restaurant where you've been given a knife and fork, eat only one of the buns; that's plenty of bread.
- If you're eating a burger at a restaurant that offers lettuce or similar nonbread wraps, give it a go.

In short, you can use your daily weigh-in to determine the number of splurges (mini-feasts/mini-fasts) you can have per week. The more you practice this habit, the more you will understand what your body needs and, more important, what it doesn't need. As we've just explained, the answer to the question of how many splurges you can get away with each week will depend on whether you need to lose weight or just maintain your current weight. If you're in weight loss mode, you're most likely going to have to stick to one splurge a week.

When framing this behavioral best practice, we were inspired by a rule put forth by the famous investor Warren Buffett, who advised that people should make no more than twenty investments over the course of their life. When describing this idea, Buffett uses the analogy of a punch card.[9] Each time you make an investment, you punch one of your allocated slots, so if you get to make only twenty investment decisions over the course of your life, you'll do your best to make sure that each decision is sound.

Part of the brilliance of Buffett's punch card analogy is that it urges you to think very carefully about each investment. We want you to think about food the same way. You get to splurge only once or twice a week, so make sure those meals count. Keeping this in mind will help you resist temptation when, faced with a craving at lunch on a Tuesday, you remember that giving in and heading to McDonald's to eat a Big Mac by yourself will mean forfeiting your chance to have dinner with your best friend at that new neighborhood barbecue place on Friday night. Clearly, one of these meals is much more valuable to you than the other. As a rule, and keeping in mind what we said at the start of this chapter about the role of feasting in society, commit to always making your splurges social.

We'd encourage you to reflect for a moment: What are your favorite foods? What are your favorite restaurants? You shouldn't have to cut them out completely. If you understand the gist of this chapter, you're still allowed to have your favorite foods occasionally, as long as you cut out all of the other bad stuff. Do you really enjoy the loaded chili cheese nachos at Applebee's? Is the Bloomin' Onion at Outback Steakhouse really your favorite dish? If your answer is yes, then by all means prioritize a carefree meal at Applebee's or Outback over a less enjoyable but equally fattening alternative; just don't do both. If you don't count such dishes among your top ten favorite foods, stay away and use those extra calories on something you truly enjoy.

Having limited your splurges per week to one or two, you'll quickly realize that there's nothing worse than wasting calories on a big meal that you don't particularly like. Even if you regret the splurge, it still counts against your weekly allowance, and even though you may skip a meal to counter its effects, there's roughly a fifty-fifty chance you'll still be up on the scale the next morning.

If you're compelled to attend the occasional (or even frequent) lunch or dinner at a place you wouldn't choose

CONCLUSION

When we started developing the principles of the Economists' Diet, we began with the fundamental observation that thin people behave differently than overweight and obese people. And we should know: as two formerly obese guys, we've done the hard work it requires to achieve and maintain a healthy weight. Most diet books have a simple narrative: "If you just do this one thing, then you'll lose weight and feel great," but we never found such quick-fix solutions. If only life were so easy!

At the same time, we understand that our advice to just eat less is easier said than done. We hope that by explaining the rationale behind each of our behavioral best practices, we've inspired you to think differently about your relationship with food. We believe that if you commit fully to our principles, you will succeed in losing weight. To put it bluntly, there's nothing special about you; your body behaves like that of every other human on the planet. If we can lose weight, so can you.

To help galvanize you to get started, here's a quick summary of the six core microhabits outlined in this book. At the end of the book, you'll find a list of twenty-five additional microhabits we've recommended you adopt. Think of this as a sort of cheat sheet as you set about putting the Economists' Diet into practice.

1. *Weigh Yourself Every Morning.* If you don't own a modern digital scale, run out and buy one right now. While many have argued that this habit can be demotivating, we know the opposite to be the case. By seeing your number on the scale every day, you will come to understand how your eating habits affect your weight—for good or for ill—and will therefore stay motivated to make the right decisions as you go about your day. The daily weigh-in will also help you manage your hunger pangs. Sure, you'll fall off the diet wagon from time to time, satisfying your craving for chips or pizza even though your rational mind says you shouldn't. But getting back on the scale each morning will keep these impulses in check and enable you to eat less over the long term.

2. *Eat Only One Square Meal a Day.* This doesn't mean you shouldn't eat three times a day; after all, there's a lot of cultural pressure to eat breakfast, lunch, and dinner. Just be aware that eating three *square* meals a day is a convention that has passed its sell-by date. Given our lifestyles and the portion inflation associated with the food processing revolution, two out of three of our daily meals should be light. The easiest way to imagine a square meal is to think of a meal consisting of grilled meat and two

vegetable sides. You'll need to experiment with your body, using a scale to fully gain an intuitive understanding of what a square meal looks like.

3. Be Calorie Conscious. A working knowledge of how many calories you're consuming is going to make weight loss a whole lot easier. And while we don't recommend counting calories (it's way too much of a grind), we do recommend that you be calorie conscious. As a reminder, all we really mean by this is that you should select lower-calorie foods when you have calorie information at hand. If you find yourself at McDonald's, and it's not a special occasion, then use the calorie information to guide you toward a cheeseburger (310 calories) instead of a Big Mac (560 calories).

4. Don't Waste Money on Fad Diets or Diet Foods. Fruits, salads, and vegetables are healthy; we doubt you need us to tell you that. But if you're like we used to be, you might have been conned into believing that certain foods are healthier or more slimming than they actually are, regardless of how much of them you eat. We don't put any stock in foods that claim to be "low fat," "diet," and so on. We're skeptical of such claims and think they distract from the real issue at hand, which is that most of us simply eat too much.

5. Limit Variety in Your Diet. Variety may keep life interesting, but if you're indulging in many different types of food all the time, you're probably paying for it on the scale. Humans naturally love to eat, and when presented with a lot of choice, we want to try a bit of everything. However, if you keep your diet relatively homogenous—sticking to a few healthy and simple meals in rotation—you will end up eating less. This doesn't mean all your meals need to be tasteless; it's just about getting used to a smaller number of options. It goes without saying that reducing the number of times you eat out each week is an essential part of limiting variety.

6. *Adopt a Mini-Feast/Mini-Fast Lifestyle.* No dieter wants to feel like he's received a prison sentence, and any diet that permanently banishes your favorite dishes or prohibits the occasional splurge isn't going to work in the long run. If you absolutely love a good burger and fries (we both do), then you've got to make room for that. In order to accommodate the occasional feast, you need to adopt a strategy of skipping the meal before or after the splurge. In our experience, it's easier to splurge at lunch and skip dinner than to fast during the day in advance of a large evening meal.

THE POWER OF PERSONAL RESPONSIBILITY

Throughout this book, we have argued that we, as individuals, need to take personal responsibility for our health rather than make excuses or rely on others to do it for us. That's why each and every one of our microhabits is directed toward the dieter, not toward, say, food manufacturers or the government. Does that mean we oppose more government intervention or regulation in the food business? Not necessarily, but we are pragmatists. We know that as long as we live in an age of abundance (which, we imagine, will be the case for a long, long time), we will always be confronted with the opportunity to eat more than we should. Therefore, we accept that it is up to us to make sure that we don't.

Earlier in the book, we applauded the US Food and Drug Administration for forcing restaurant chains to provide calorie information about the food they sell. Such information can help nudge us toward making better decisions, though we also recognize that disclosure standards can always be improved. For instance, thanks to scientific studies and personal experimentation, we know that too many carbohydrates pile on the pounds. As such, the FDA could help advance the development of a "weight-gain score" that would take into account not just calories but also the likelihood that a particular food will cause you to gain weight. This score, when displayed on all the food we buy, whether in restaurants or grocery stores, could go a long way toward guiding our decision making. Following on from this, we support government-funded nutritional educational programs aimed at all ages, from schoolkids to retirees. Of course, these programs needn't be overly complicated: something as simple as "Eat more salad" combined with an explanation of how much sugar is too much sugar would represent a good starting point.

But as we discussed in chapter 3, history has shown us that disclosure isn't the great panacea that we wish it were; often people don't know what to do with the data, or they just plain ignore them. If a government really wanted to reverse our obesity epidemic, it could consider more direct intervention, like a tax. Why not, for instance, place a tax on junk food that, as with cigarettes, discourages consumption? While not widespread, there are countries that have imposed such taxes: Denmark, Finland, France, Hungary, and Mexico, to name a few. In the United States, taxes on sugar-sweetened beverages and energy-dense processed foods exist in the Navajo Nation and in the city of Berkeley, California.[1]

It's certainly not an unreasonable approach and has been explored by the bipartisan US think tank, the Tax Policy Center, in a 2015 research report titled *Should We Tax Unhealthy Foods and Drinks?*[2] The paper explains that, for such a tax to work effectively, it would have to be levied on sugar content so as to encourage producers to reduce the amount of sugar in existing drinks and develop new, less-sugary alternatives. And because businesses do their best to pass the cost of taxes on to consumers, higher prices could also send consumers in search of healthier options.

Based on experiences around the world, the authors estimate "that moderate taxes on sugar-sweetened beverages could reduce obesity rates by 1 to 4 percentage points in the United States." But with the obesity rate as it is at present, around 36 percent, they admit that the benefits would be modest. Moreover, such a tax would likely disproportionately punish poorer segments of society that don't have the money to switch to better, and thus more expensive, alternatives. Indeed, when the City of Berkeley imposed a one-cent tax per fluid ounce on sugary drinks, the effect was relatively muted because manufacturers chose to only partly pass on the tax to consumers. To have a large effect, the tax would have to be very large indeed.[3]

Whether moderate or punitive, any proposed taxes on sugar would likely infuriate the US public, which cherishes its freedom of choice. After all, this is the same reason why more direct attempts at intervention in the United States have failed. Take, for instance, New York City's attempt to prohibit the sale of sweetened beverages in sizes larger than sixteen ounces. As a policy, it is entirely consistent with our view that you should resist all upselling and avoid drinking your calories. All the same, the courts put a stop to New York's plans, saying the city didn't have the authority to limit public choice. Legal arguments aside, we view the court's decision as a reflection of public opinion: government prohibitions on what we ingest are probably never going to gain favor, as people guard their freedoms too fiercely to accept government controls. And even where governments have freer rein and more support in such matters, we suspect that outright bans on giant-sized sodas represent a step outside their policy comfort zone.

We'd certainly welcome a full, open, and mature debate on the role of government in tackling obesity, and it may be that the tide of public opinion will change in the future. But we will probably be waiting a long time—too long for many people currently struggling with their weight. Just note, for instance, President Barack Obama's response to a question from TV comedian and political pundit Bill Maher in one of his last interviews before leaving office. Maher suggested that the government is "afraid to ask the people to eat better." He continued, "You know, the phrase was 'Yes, we can,' and I feel like they're not pulling their weight on the 'we,' and it's a partnership with government. Eat better, vote more, learn something."

Obama's response: "You know, I actually think that part of the pitch I've made throughout my campaign and throughout my presidency is exactly that: change doesn't come from on high. That if you're waiting for Congress, then you're going to wait a long time." And this coming from a president who is considered by some to be a fan of big government!

In short, we have no choice but to accept that the battle to lose weight and keep it off is a personal one. In framing this book around the principle of taking personal responsibility, we have also made it clear that there is no single magic bullet that can solve weight issues overnight. On the contrary, we have stressed that such offerings are a mirage that actually undermine our ability to lose weight. Achieving your target weight is a long-term project; maintaining it, a forever project. Still, in saying this, we are not suggesting that it all comes down to willpower. As you follow our microhabits, you will notice that they become easier to practice over time, meaning you don't always have to rely on willpower alone.

Of course, in order for dieters to form these habits in the first place, coming off autopilot eating in the process, they will need to use their powers of self-awareness and self-control. We have wondered, therefore, if one of the underlying reasons so many people have trouble losing weight is because they lack the willpower to commit to a permanent diet. In thinking about this, we have come to the conclusion that, in some cases, diet failure may be one symptom of a greater problem that we all face in the abundant society: that of instant gratification. We've become so used to having what we want when we want it, playing into marketing gimmicks that promise us amazing results without the hassle, that we assume there must be an easier alternative to losing weight than the hard and sometimes painful work of dieting.

This became evident to us when discussing the Economists' Diet with a friend of ours who has struggled with obesity for a long time. At first, he was very interested in what we had to say, and many of our ideas were new to him, especially our insistence on the daily weigh-in. We thought we had found another convert: a future success story we could one day brag about when touting the benefits of the Economists' Diet.

Then we mentioned the necessity of hunger. We told him that, in order to lose weight, he was going to have to become comfortable feeling hungry, that he would have to resist the urge to satisfy every sensation or pang as soon as it hit. Apparently, this was where he drew the line. He said that he simply couldn't cope with feeling hungry, and therefore our ideas wouldn't work for him. Of course, as you know by now, having read to the end of this book, we were not asking him to sign up for a lifetime of discomfort; the point of the Economists' Diet, after all, is to make changes to your behavior that over time become second nature. But this particular friend was, in essence, looking for a way to lose weight without having to exert any effort.

We took his comment seriously and have suggested ways we hope will help you overcome the feeling of hunger. But at the end of the day, we will say the same thing to any overweight or obese person, including this friend: if you are unwilling to experience hunger from time to time, you will never lose weight. To achieve anything of value in life requires some element of sacrifice.

While our economy has succeeded because of, not in spite of, its freedoms, the consumer ethic it has spawned can sometimes undermine our ability to think long term. So many of our economic problems arise from our unwillingness to consider our future needs, exacerbated, of course, by the impossibility of predicting the future with a high degree of certainty. The result seems to be that, rather than being sovereign consumers playing a role, alongside entrepreneurs, in deciding what products we want and need, we have, in many instances, become beleaguered consumers, swept up in a tsunami of products, less able than we should be to make rational choices that best suit our needs.

This, surely, is the central theme of our own personal stories of weight gain. Neither of us wanted to be obese, but for many years, we were incapable of taking back control over our bodies. Yet doing just that—coming off autopilot eating and taking back control—offers so many benefits. On the one hand, more stronger-willed consumers would be good for all. Reasserting our need to eat less and eat more healthily would help foster a food industry inclined to better serve our long-term interests. Businesses, after all, want to make money, and they'll ultimately provide what we demand of them.

On the other hand, on a personal level, reestablishing control over your body is an inexorable part of making you a more authentic version of yourself: an outcome of consciously made choices, less a passive reflection of the world around you. Indeed, as no less a philosopher than Friedrich Nietzsche has stated, overcoming outside influences and determining the person you actually are require you "*not* to react immediately to a stimulus, but to have restraining, stock-taking instincts in one's control."[4]

Of course we are mere mortals. We will always stray, we will always succumb, and we will always celebrate an occasion to feast and be merry. But in general, we can win the battle that takes place in our minds, and resist temptation more often than we give into it. It takes practice and time to get there, and it isn't easy, but the benefits that come with refusal and restraint are far greater than just weight loss. Keeping one's instincts under control and remaining aware of the forces at work around you paves the way to a clearer and more enlightened perspective on who you really are.

CELEBRATING SUCCESS

Throughout *The Economists' Diet* we have tried to do three specific things. First and foremost, we have provided practical suggestions based on various principles of economics that will help you achieve lasting weight loss results. Second, we have shown how our age of abundance has directly contributed to our growing collective weight problem. This is important because it emphasizes the need to self-impose eating austerity—pretending food is scarce even when it isn't—in order to deal with the seemingly endless opportunities to eat whatever and whenever you want. Third, we have shared our own personal weight loss narratives in order to show you that we know what we're talking about; if what we're saying worked for us, it can work for you.

Another reason we thought it important to share our stories with you is because we hope they will inspire you and keep you motivated as you begin your diet. To this end, we've spent a lot of time talking about our experiences of dieting. But now that we've come to the end of the book, we want to leave you on a lighter note, by sharing some of the joys we've experienced since committing to the Economists' Diet. First Chris, then Rob.

CHRIS'S SUCCESS STORY

This is a story about shopping. It might seem odd coming at the end of a book about dieting in which we've consistently urged you not to buy into the general consumerist mentality. But not all consumerism is bad! In fact, when done for the right reasons, it can be a form of celebration.

But first, a little context.

When I started my diet, I wore size 38 pants. By the end of the diet—and, I should add, to this day—I had a 32-inch waist. When I first started dieting, I knew how much weight I needed to lose, but I didn't know how this was going to affect my body shape or clothing size. In fact, as I began to lose weight, I never really noticed that my pants were getting too big. I do remember having to punch a couple of extra holes in my belt, but it never occurred to me that I must look really silly in my jeans.

I dieted for around eighteen months, and because the weight loss was slow and steady, I never had one particular moment in which I saw myself in the mirror and thought, "Holy cow! I'm thin!" This was probably helped by the fact that, at around the same time, I left the world of finance and returned to graduate school. After years of wearing suits, I was enjoying a newfound "schleppyness" and basically lived in some old, increasingly oversized jeans.

By January 2006, two years after starting the diet, I was looking quite ridiculous in my old clothes. I looked like a kid in ill-fitting hand-me-downs. Also, thanks to my baggy britches, I appeared to have absolutely no butt at all. Luckily, it was around this time that I started dating Nadia, the woman who would eventually become my wife. She must have agreed to go out with me because I wooed her with my charisma and witty personality, because it certainly had nothing to do with my impeccable sense of style. In fact, according to her, I looked like someone who had given up "real" work and couldn't give two hoots about his appearance. She was willing to cut me a bit of slack at the beginning of our relationship, but before long, she decided that even if *I* didn't care too much about the way I looked, *she* certainly did. I had become, to use the current vernacular, a "fixer-upper."

One afternoon Nadia suggested we take a trip to the Gap on Oxford Street in London so I could buy what she called "the basics." The result was a hectic but productive hourlong shopping session in which Nadia threw various jeans, shirts, and sweaters over the top of the dressing room door for me to try on. Previously, shopping expeditions had been painful reminders of how fat I had become. Now, however, I found I rather enjoyed the experience. In fact, I discovered I could actually buy some pants that made me look relatively slim. I certainly wasn't an Adonis, but with the new clothes on, I felt pretty damn good about what I saw in the mirror.

By the end of the trip, my efforts to secure the basics

had led me to purchase an entire new wardrobe. I remember how, as I paid for my new clothes, the cashier gave me a business card with the name and number of a personal shopping consultant on it. She said that if I ever felt the need to buy a new wardrobe again, I should call this number, and someone could assist me with my needs. I replied that it wasn't very likely, thanked her, smiled, and walked away.

Looking back on that day, I realize I couldn't have planned a more perfect way to celebrate what I had achieved. I'm so happy I got to have that experience with the woman I love, and I hope each and every one of you gets to experience something similar.

It also made me realize that I could never go back to my old weight again. I couldn't face the prospect of having to buy yet another new wardrobe, this time as my waistline got bigger and bigger. Throughout this book, we have insisted that the daily weigh-in is the best way to monitor and control your weight, but another signal that you're going off track is the feeling of your clothes getting tight. It's horrible. If it happens, use it as motivation to get things back under control immediately.

In writing this, I've also come to realize that, in referring me to a personal shopper, the cashier at the Gap must have thought there was a chance I'd come back in to replace my wardrobe one day. Of course, she didn't know that this shopping spree was the culmination of two years of hard work, not a concession to my shopping addiction. To her, I was just another regular guy who was willing to plunk down a few hundred quid for some sensible shirts and classic-cut jeans.

Once I lost the weight and debuted the new clothes, the reaction I got from old colleagues and acquaintances who hadn't seen me in a while was remarkable. I had no idea I looked so different from a couple of years prior. One former colleague told me that I seemed to have lost half my face; another, whom I had sat next to at work for three years, quite literally didn't recognize me when I bumped into him on a train. Both were, of course, very complimentary about my new look, though I can't imagine what I must have looked like to them back when I was obese. I have to say I hadn't expected such a reaction, but when I look at photos of the old me, I can see that an enormous transformation had taken place.

ROB'S SUCCESS STORY

Like Chris, I can relate to the experience of buying new clothes. At my heaviest, I bought a custom suit, which at the time, like all custom-made suits, "fit me like a glove." These days, if I try it on, I look like a clown.

At my heaviest, I had a 50-inch chest; now I wear a 42-inch blazer. It's amazing to think that I lost 8 inches across my chest—and nearly as much around my waist. I've enjoyed replacing my wardrobe, but I did it incrementally instead of all at once like Chris.

Yet as much as I enjoy fitting into smaller clothes, the

biggest benefit I've gained from losing weight has been to my health. When I was nearing my highest weight, my office happened to have a health screening clinic that entitled participants to pay a reduced health insurance premium (no matter what the results were). When I first saw the nurse that morning, she asked if I was nervous. I said, "No. Why?" She looked at me with concern and said, "Your blood pressure is 165 over 90." I didn't appreciate what that meant at the time, and she said it was probably a fluke and asked me to come back later that morning. When I returned, the results were even worse: 180 over 90!

The nurse called her supervisor, and they both agreed that I needed to seek immediate medical attention. (A normal blood pressure is 120 over 80.) The nurse, in consultation with her supervisor, wanted to call an ambulance for me and said that I needed to head straight to the hospital, as I was in "imminent danger of having a heart attack." As frightening as that was, I asked her if I could go to my primary care physician instead, under the care of my wife. She relented but made me sign a waiver saying I wouldn't hold her liable if anything happened, since I was disregarding her timely medical advice. My doctor recorded a similar blood pressure and immediately put me on medication. It took several visits to calibrate my dosage, but we eventually settled on a 20-milligram pill of lisinopril, an ACE inhibitor, twice a day—a fairly aggressive treatment regimen for somebody in his midthirties.

After I lost a staggering seventy-five pounds, my doctor was so blown away that she gave me a high five and a hug in her office one afternoon. She suggested we experiment with reducing my blood pressure medicine, and, after some experimentation, we eventually determined that I didn't need it anymore. (Never stop taking medication without consulting your physician!)

I still monitor my blood pressure periodically, and I continue to be amazed at how well I've done. My diastolic blood pressure, the lower reading and the more important of the two that measures the pressure in the arteries when the heart rests between beats, usually comes in at 65 or 70 (the lower the better, within reason). I don't know if my results are typical, but the American Heart Association says that being overweight puts you at higher risks for elevated blood pressure and other cardiovascular diseases,[5] so if you're overweight and currently struggling with one of these ailments, losing weight will have a positive impact on more than just your reading on the scale.

I realize now that when I was at my most obese, I was literally putting my life in jeopardy, even after I started taking medication. And while I'm certainly happy that I lost the weight for my own sake, I'm even more glad that I can better keep up with my young and very active children—and will hopefully be able to do so for a long time to come.

While both of these stories are meant to inspire, you'll notice that Chris's is much more lighthearted than Rob's. Rob's story of lowering his blood pressure is about more than just celebrating a slimmer waistline (though that's certainly a good reason to celebrate). It's about celebrating the newfound chance to live a longer, healthier life—a life in which you will hopefully accumulate years of joyful moments.

Rob's story speaks to one of our core messages. As economists, we've argued that, ideally, we should be tallying up the costs and benefits of each and every consumption decision. Yes, we enjoy an in-the-moment splurge, but we also need to stay aware of the effects that too many splurges have on our future health. Like many economic problems, our obesity epidemic reflects an all-too-human proclivity to overvalue the present and undervalue the future. It's easily done, especially when the future is so uncertain.

But if Rob's story tells us anything, it's that the effects of years of overdoing it on your body aren't really that uncertain at all. As a dieter, when you consider the enjoyment of overeating now against the benefits of better health down the line, you're not dealing with abstract concepts such as market fluctuations or inflation. You can act with almost 100 percent certainty that your decision will have a positive impact on your health.

In order for us to successfully lose weight, we had to think long and hard about why we gained weight in the first place. As economists, we framed the problem in terms of abundance and shortsightedness, and developed our behavioral best practices in order to address the challenges that so many of us face. Even so, we didn't write

The Economists' Diet to be the last word on behavioral approaches to dieting. Of course we believe our best practices will help you lose weight, but we also believe that you're going to learn all sorts of things as you try them in your own life. We're active on Twitter (@econdiet), and we hope you'll share with us what you learn as you set about your own weight loss journeys. Tweet us your stories, your ideas, and your experiments; tweet us your weight if you want. We wish you luck. And we look forward to hearing from you.

THE ECONOMISTS' DIET CHECKLIST OF BEHAVIORAL BEST PRACTICES

SIX CORE MICROHABITS

- Weigh yourself every day.
- Eat one square meal a day.
- Be calorie conscious.
- Don't waste money on fad diets or diet food.
- Limit variety in your diet.
- Adopt a mini-feast/mini-fast lifestyle.

TWENTY-FIVE ADDITIONAL MICROHABITS

- Listen to your body's signals of hunger and fullness.
- Wait before satiating hunger.
- Seek moral support from friends and family.
- Establish meta-rules to guide future decisions about what to eat.
- Identify meals as either square, light, or a splurge, and manage your daily intake accordingly.
- Spend money on kitchen essentials, not on fancy equipment you'll never use.

THE ECONOMISTS' DIET CHECKLIST

- Keep snacks out of arm's reach; better still, resolve not to buy them in the first place.
- Stop making excuses for why you're overweight.
- Don't drink your calories.
- Use a scale to experiment with your diet; keep a food diary if it helps.
- Limit your consumption of bread, pasta, pizza, and sugar.
- Set a realistic long-term weight loss target and smaller short-term targets to keep you motivated.
- Prepare to spend about eighteen months to lose fifty pounds.
- Resist all upselling.
- Order the smallest size available.
- Be skeptical of food marketing campaigns, especially those using the word *lite*.
- Buy your groceries online when possible or make a shopping list to help curb in-store impulse purchases.
- Avoid volume-based discount stores.
- Forgo sugar and artificial sweeteners in your tea and coffee.
- Take a salad or leftovers with you for lunch at work.
- Ignore all quick fixes; be prepared to eat less food forever.
- Focus on preparing more food at home.
- Budget for special occasions and vacations: save up calories in advance, pay off calorie debts after.
- Splurge at lunch rather than at dinner.
- Choose your splurges carefully; don't waste calories on food you don't really enjoy.

ACKNOWLEDGMENTS

As any author knows, the process of writing a book from start to finish involves receiving help and guidance from innumerable people. We know that our project never would have come this far without the input of others: their thoughts, ideas, and criticisms. We'd like to thank everyone we've talked to about dieting and this book (and there are many) over the past few years.

In particular, though, we'd like to thank Melissa Sarver White for being so enthusiastic about our project from such an early stage, and for helping us turn our ideas into a book; it simply would not have happened without her. We'd also like to thank all the team at Touchstone publishers, including Cara Bedick and Lara Blackman, for all their hard work on the book. We are especially grateful for Cara's wisdom; her detailed, clear, and comprehensive feedback has added huge value, ensuring that this book offers as much practical advice to readers as possible. Finally, we'd like to express our enormous gratitude to Brooke Carey for helping us craft a book that, in the hands of two economists, easily could have been overly dry and technical.

ACKNOWLEDGMENTS

Friends, colleagues, and peers have had an enormous impact on our ideas and thoughts and in helping us navigate the world of publishing. While there really are too many to single out every person, we would like to express our enduring gratitude to Don Baptiste, Todd Henry, Susan Doyle, Bob Litan, Lisa Getter, Jesse Hamilton, Aisha Salem, Jason Arvelo, Charles Brock, Nathan Dean, Fida Hanna, Ali Abbas, David Knapp, Tim and Jo Dickson, Alun Jones, Omar Negyal, Adrian Brettle, Dan Holland, Peter Rickett, Jason Mann, Tom Kyriakoudis, Edward and Emma Griffin, Neda Semnani, Lujain Alshalfan, and Megan Paulson.

Of course, no book can be written without the support of one's loved ones.

Chris would like to thank his mother-in-law, Khawla Nimri (the world's leading authority on self-imposed austerity eating), and sister-in-law, Najat Ziyadeh, for their thoughts and ideas. As always with any of his endeavors, his brother, Richard, and parents, Ian and Pauline, provided invaluable and tireless support—when they probably had better things to do with their time than read and discuss *The Economists' Diet* for the umpteenth time. Finally, and most important, Chris would like to express his love and gratitude to his wife, Nadia, whose endless provision of love, patience, help, and ideas have made all the difference. Long before this book was born, Chris was assimilating Nadia's ideas on how to get the most enjoyment out of eating while not gaining weight.

Rob would like to thank his wife, Anne Marie, first for

putting up with the trials and tribulations that accompany successful weight loss, and then for her support while he and Chris labored over *The Economists' Diet* for nearly four years. He's thankful Anne Marie didn't kick him to the curb when he started packing his scale—and thus taking up valuable space—in their luggage before heading off on vacations. Rob has always been blessed to be supported by loving parents, Ken and Sheryln, and by his sister, Kathy, and her husband, Tim. And even though she insists on stuffing his face with homemade Chex Mix, Rob is thankful for his mother-in-law, Karen, and his wife's sister, Mary, and her brothers Andrew, Donavan, and Tyler. And he's thankful to his brother-in-law, David, for helping him to calibrate his scale in 2014.

NOTES

Introduction

1. Sherry Rauh, "Is Fat the New Normal?," WebMD, www
   .webmd.com/diet/obesity/features/is-fat-the-new-nor
   mal#1.
2. According to Livestrong.com, "Up to 90 percent of teen-
   agers diet regularly, and up to 50 percent of younger kids
   have tried a diet at some point," in Tammy Dray, "Facts
   & Statistics About Dieting," Livestrong.com, July 1, 2015,
   www.livestrong.com/article/390541-facts-statistics-about-
   dieting.
3. Vanessa K. Ridaura et al., "Gut Microbiota from Twins
   Discordant for Obesity Modulate Metabolism in Mice,"
   Science 341 (September 6, 2013): doi: 10.1126/sci
   ence.1241214.
4. Susan Teitelbaum et al., "Associations Between Phthal-
   ate Metabolite Urinary Concentrations and Body Size
   Measure in New York City Children," *Environmental
   Research* 112 (January 2012): 186–93: doi: 10.1016/j.en
   vres.2011.12.006.
5. For a summary of recent scientific findings on causes of
   obesity, see Sandra Aamodt, *Why Diets Make Us Fat: The
   Unintended Consequences of Our Obsession with Weight
   Loss* (New York: Current, 2016), 83–156.
6. Gary Taubes, *Why We Get Fat and What to Do About It*
   (New York: Random House: Anchor Books, 2011), 10.

NOTES

7. Aamodt, *Why Diets Make Us Fat*, 130–35.
8. Cheryl D. Fryar, Margaret D. Carroll, and Cynthia L. Ogden, "Prevalence of Overweight, Obesity, and Extreme Obesity Among Adults: United States, Trends 1960–1962 Through 2009–2010," Centers for Disease Control and Prevention, National Center for Health Statistics, www.cdc.gov/nchs/data/hestat/obesity_adult_09_10/obesity_adult_09_10.htm.
9. Ibid.
10. World Health Organization, "Obesity and Overweight Factsheet," last modified June 2016, www.who.int/mediacentre/factsheets/fs311/en.
11. Ibid.
12. "Global Database on Body Mass Index: An Interactive Surveillance Tool for Monitoring Nutrition Transition," World Health Organization, http://apps.who.int/bmi/index.jsp.
13. David M. Cutler, Edward L. Glaeser, and Jesse M. Shapiro, "Why Have Americans Become More Obese?," *Journal of Economic Perspectives* 17 (Summer 2003): 93–118: doi: 10.1257/089533003769204371.
14. The Maddison-Project, www.ggdc.net/maddison/maddison-project/home.htm, 2013 version.
15. "Serving Sizes and Portions," National Heart, Lung, and Blood Institute, www.nhlbi.nih.gov/health/educational/wecan/eat-right/distortion.htm.
16. John Maynard Keynes, *The General Theory of Employment, Interest and Money* (1936; repr., London: Macmillan Press, 1973), 96.
17. Cynthia L. Ogden and Margaret D. Carroll, "Prevalence of Overweight, Obesity, and Extreme Obesity Among Adults: United States, Trends 1960–1962 Through 2007–2008," Table 2, Centers for Disease Control and Prevention, National Center for Health Statistics, June 2010, www.cdc.gov/nchs/data/hestat/obesity_adult_07. . ./obesity_adult_07_08.pdf.
18. Adam Smith, *The Wealth of Nations* (1776; repr., Amherst, NY: Prometheus Books, 1991), 174.

19. Tibor Scitovsky, *The Joyless Economy: The Psychology of Human Satisfaction* (New York: Oxford University Press, 1992), 59–63.

Chapter 1.
Scarcity (Why You Need to Weigh Yourself Every Day)

1. Erin Fothergill et al., "Persistent Metabolic Adaptation 6 Years After 'The Biggest Loser' Competition," *Obesity* 24, (August 2016): 1612–19, http://onlinelibrary.wiley.com/doi/10.1002/oby.21538/full.
2. Sendhil Mullainathan and Eldar Shafir, *Scarcity: The New Science of Having Less and How It Defines Our Lives* (New York: Picador, 2014), 115, 155.
3. Ibid., 39–66.
4. Lamar Salter, "How to Trick Your Brain and Control Your Impulses," Business Insider, last modified August 12, 2015, www.businessinsider.com/trick-brain-control-eating-im pulses-psychology-2015-7.
5. Mona Chalabi, "How Much Weight Will I Gain at Christmas and How Long Will It Take to Lose It?," *Guardian*, December 20, 2016, www.theguardian.com/news/reali ty-check/2013/dec/20/how-much-weight-will-i-gain-at-christmas-and-how-long-will-it-take-to-lose-it.
6. Ibid.
7. Carly R. Pacanowski and David A. Levitsky, "Frequent Self-Weighing and Visual Feedback for Weight Loss in Overweight Adults," *Journal of Obesity* (June 2015), https://www.hindawi.com/journals/jobe/2015/763680.
8. Ibid. The study was conducted with two groups of patients: one group, randomly selected, spent two years following a method in which the individuals adjust downwards their food intake based on feedback from the daily weigh-in. The second group adopted this method after the first year. A significant difference in weight loss was observed over the first year between the two groups. In the second year, the first group

of individuals maintained their weight loss, the second group caught up.

9. Krishna Ramanujan, "Keeping Track of Weight Daily May Tip Scale in Your Favor," *Cornell Chronicle*, June 12, 2015, www.news.cornell.edu/stories/2015/06/keeping-track-weight-daily-may-tip-scale-your-favor.

Chapter 2.
Abundance (Busting the Myth of Three Square Meals a Day)

1. "Estimated Calorie Needs per Day by Age, Gender, and Physical Activity Level," US Department of Agriculture, https://www.cnpp.usda.gov/sites/default/. . ./EstimatedCalorieNeedsPerDayTable.pdf.

2. "US Personal Saving Rate," Federal Reserve Bank of St. Louis, https://fred.stlouisfed.org/series/PSAVERT/.

3. Abigail Carroll, *Three Squares: The Invention of the American Meal* (New York: Basic Books, 2013), 2–5.

4. Denise Winterman, "Breakfast, Lunch, and Dinner: Have We Always Eaten Them?," *BBC News Magazine*, November 15, 2012, www.bbc.co.uk/news/magazine-20243692.

5. Anneli Rufus, "There Is No Biological Reason to Eat Three Meals a Day—So Why Do We Do It?," *AlterNet*, September 23, 2011, www.alternet.org/story/152486/there_is_no_biological_reason_to_eat_three_meals_a_day_--_so_why_do_we_do_it.

6. Carroll, *Three Squares*, 7.

7. Ibid., see chapter 3.

8. Ibid., see chapter 5, especially pages 125–26.

9. Ibid., see chapter 6.

10. *Eating for Victory: Healthy Home Front Cooking on War Rations* (London: Michael O'Mara Books, 2007).

11. Fothergill et al., "Persistent Metabolic Adaptation," 1612–19, http://onlinelibrary.wiley.com/doi/10.1002/oby.21538/full.

12. Ibid.

NOTES

13. World Health Organization, "Overweight (Body Mass Index ≥ 25), Age-Standardized (%), Estimates by Country," Global Health Observatory data repository, http://apps.who.int/gho/data/node.main.A897A?lang=en.

Chapter 3.
Data (Be Calorie Conscious, Not a Calorie Counter)

1. "Estimated Calorie Needs per Day by Age, Gender and Physical Activity Level," US Department of Agriculture, https://www.cnpp.usda.gov/sites/default/. . ./. . ./Estimated CalorieNeedsPerDayTable.pdf.
2. Aaron E. Carroll, "The Failure of Calorie Counts on Menus," *New York Times*, November 30, 2015, www.nytimes.com/2015/12/01/upshot/more-menus-have-calorie-labeling-but-obesity-rate-remains-high.html?_r=0.
3. See US Department of Agriculture's Branded Food Products Database: https://ndb.nal.usda.gov/ndb/foods.
4. Lorien E. Urban et al., "The Accuracy of Stated Energy Contents of Reduced-Energy, Commercially Prepared Foods," *Journal of the American Dietetic Association* 110, (January 2010): 116–23, doi: 10.1016/j.jada.2009.10.003.
5. Ibid.
6. Lauren Gensler, "Oprah Pays $43 Million for Weight Watchers Stake, Stock Spikes," *Forbes*, October 19, 2015, www.forbes.com/sites/laurengensler/2015/10/19/weight-watchers-oprah-winfrey/#2ac48ad17b3b.
7. Susan A. Jebb et al., "Primary Care Referral to a Commercial Provider for Weight Loss Treatment Versus Standard Care: A Randomised Controlled Trial," *Lancet* 378, no. 9801 (October 22, 2011): 1485–92, www.thelancet.com/journals/lancet/article/PIIS0140-6736(11)61344-5/fulltext.
8. M. R. Lowe, K. Miller-Kovach, and S. Phelan, "Weight-Loss Maintenance in Overweight Individuals One to Five Years Following Successful Completion of a Commercial Weight Loss Program," *International Journal of Obesity* 25

(March 2001): 325–31, www.nature.com/ijo/journal/v25/n3/full/0801521a.html.

9. Ashley Collman, "High school science teacher who lost 60 pounds eating McDonald's for every meal is now a brand ambassador for the company," *Daily Mail*, last modified May 12, 2015, http://www.dailymail.co.uk/news/article-3077366/High-school-science-teacher-lost-60-pounds-eating-McDonald-s-meal-brand-ambassador-company.html.

Chapter 4.
Buyer Beware (Don't Waste Time or Money on the Diet Industrial Complex)

1. Daniel Kahneman, *Thinking Fast and Slow* (2011; repr., London: Penguin, 2012), 105.
2. Ibid., 21.
3. German Lopez, "A Medium Cup of Coca-Cola Has More Added Sugar Than You Should Drink in a Day," Vox, last modified November 24, 2014, www.vox.com/xpress/2014/11/24/7275749/coke-sugar-cup.
4. "Guidance for Industry: A Food Labeling Guide (9. Appendix A: Definitions of Nutrient Content Claims)," US Food and Drug Administration, last modified August 20, 2015, www.fda.gov/Food/GuidanceRegulation/GuidanceDocumentsRegulatoryInformation/LabelingNutrition/ucm064911.htm.
5. Cristin E. Kearns, Laura A. Schmidt, and Stanton A. Glantz, "Sugar Industry and Coronary Heart Disease Research: A Historical Analysis of Internal Industry Documents," *JAMA Internal Medicine* 176 (November 2016): 1680–85, doi: 10.1001/jamainternmed.2016.5394.
6. Ibid.
7. Ibid.
8. Anahad O'Connor, "Research Group Funded by Coca-Cola to Disband," *New York Times*, December 1, 2015,

Well (blog), https://well.blogs.nytimes.com/2015/12/01/research-group-funded-by-coca-cola-to-disband/?_r=1.

9. Elizabeth Lopatto and Michelle Fay Cortez, "Obesity Drops Among Young Children in U.S., Report Says," Bloomberg, last modified February 26, 2014, www.bloomberg.com/news/2014-02-25/obesity-drops-among-young-children-in-u-s-report-says.html.

10. Mary Story and Simone French, "Food Advertising and Marketing Directed at Children and Adolescents in the US," *International Journal of Behavioral Nutrition and Physical Activity* 1 (February 10, 2004), table 6: Chronology of Key Events in US Regulations on Advertising to Children, https://ijbnpa.biomedcentral.com/articles/10.1186/1479-5868-1-3.

11. Meghan Casserly, "Beyoncé's $50 Million Pepsi Deal Takes Creative Cues from Jay Z," *Forbes*, December 10, 2012, www.forbes.com/sites/meghancasserly/2012/12/10/beyonce-knowles-50-million-pepsi-deal-takes-creative-cues-from-jay-z/#94dc5343bf8b.

12. Paco Underhill, *Why We Buy: The Science of Shopping* (New York: Simon & Schuster, 1999).

13. David R. Bell, Daniel Corsten, and George Knox, "From Point of Purchase to Path to Purchase: How Preshopping Factors Drive Unplanned Buying," *Journal of Marketing* 75 (January 2011): 31–45, http://journals.ama.org/doi/abs/10.1509/jmkg.75.1.31?code=amma-site&journalCode=jmkg.

14. "Not on the List? The Truth About Impulse Purchases," Knowledge@Wharton, last modified January 7, 2009, http://knowledge.wharton.upenn.edu/article/not-on-the-list-the-truth-about-impulse-purchases.

15. Kahneman, *Thinking Fast and Slow,* 41, 105.

16. Gary W. Evans and Jennifer Rosenbaum, "Self-Regulation and the Income-Achievement Gap," *Early Childhood Research Quarterly* 23 (4th Quarter 2008): 504–14, www.sciencedirect.com/science/article/pii/S0885200608000549.

17. Walter Mischel, Ebbe B. Ebbesen, and Antonette Raskoff Zeiss, "Cognitive and Attentional Mechanisms in Delay of

Gratification," *Journal of Personality and Social Psychology* 21 (February 1972): 204–18, PMID: 2658056.

18. Tanya R. Schlam et al., "Preschoolers' Delay of Gratification Predicts Their Body Mass 30 Years Later," *Journal of Pediatrics* 162 (January 2013): 90–93, doi: 10.1016/j.j peds.2012.06.049.

19. Janet Polivy, "Psychological Consequences of Food Restriction," *Journal of the American Dietetic Association* 96 (June 1996): 589–92, doi: 10.1016/S002-8223(96)00161-7.

20. Sharon P. G. Fowler, Ken Williams, and Helen P. Hazuda, "Diet Soda Intake Is Associated with Long-Term Increases in Waist Circumference in a Bi-Ethnic Cohort of Older Adults: The San Antonio Longitudinal Study of Aging," *Journal of American Geriatrics Society* 63 (April 2015): 708–15, www.ncbi.nlm.nih.gov/pmc/articles/PMC4498394.

21. Mary Squillace, "10 Reasons to Give Up Diet Soda," Health, www.health.com/health/gallery/0,,20739512,00 .html.

22. See, for instance, Toby Amidor, "Veggie Chips: Are They Healthy," Food Network, Health Tips, Health Eats (blogs), last modified October 10, 2011, http://blog.foodnetwork .com/healthyeats/2011/10/10/veggie-chips-are-they-healthy.

Chapter 5.
Equilibrium (Variety May Be the Spice of Life, but It's Also Making You Fat)

1. Carl Menger, *Principles of Economics,* trans. James Dingwall and Bert F. Hoselitz (Glencoe, IL: Free Press, 1950), 127.

2. Richard G. Lipsey and K. Alec Chrystal, *Principles of Economics* (Oxford: Oxford University Press, 1999), 89.

3. "Institute of Medicine–Estimated Energy Requirement

(EER)," Global RPh, www.globalrph.com/estimated_ energy_requirement.htm.

Chapter 6.
Budgeting (How to Splurge and Still Lose Weight)

1. William Poundstone, *Prisoner's Dilemma: John von Neumann, Game Theory, and the Puzzle of the Bomb* (1992; repr., New York: Anchor Books, 1993), 118.
2. Tibor Scitovsky, *The Joyless Economy: The Psychology of Human Satisfaction* (New York: Oxford University Press, 1992), 65–66.
3. Kathleen M. Zelman, "Diet Truth or Myth: Eating at Night Causes Weight Gain," WebMD, http://www.webmd.com/ diet/features/diet-truth-myth-eating-night-causes-weight-gain#1
4. David Stipp, "How Intermittent Fasting Might Help You Live a Longer and Healthier Life," *Scientific American*, January 1, 2013, www.scientificamerican.com/article/how-intermittent-fasting-might-help-you-live-longer-healthier-life.
5. Leonie K. Heilbronn and Eric Ravussin, "Calorie Restriction and Aging: Review of the Literature and Implications for Studies in Humans," *American Journal of Clinical Nutrition* 78 (September 2003): 361–69, http:// ajcn.nutrition.org/content/78/3/361.abstract?ijkey=7ac6b 23639d259241484ea7fad8a44db1ef28be8&keytype2=tf _ipsecsha&cited-by=yes&legid=ajcn;78/3/361.
6. Ibid.
7. Ricki J. Colman et al., "Caloric Restriction Reduces Age-Related and All-Cause Mortality in Rhesus Monkeys," *Nature Communications* 5 (April 14, 2014): doi: 10.1038 /ncomms4557.
8. Ibid.
9. John G. Taft, "You Only Live Once, So Do It Warren Buffett's Way," *Huffington Post*, October 28, 2014, www.huff

ingtonpost.com/john-g-taft/you-only-live-once-do-it-_b
_5725112.html.

Conclusion

1. Donald Marron, Maeve E. Gearing, and John Iselin, *Should We Tax Unhealthy Foods and Drinks?* (Washington, DC: Tax Policy Center, Urban Institute and Brookings Institution, December 2015), 1, www.taxpolicycenter.org/publi cations/should-we-tax-unhealthy-foods-and-drinks/full.
2. Ibid.
3. Ibid., 2.
4. Friedrich Nietzsche, *Twilight of the Idols* (1889; repr., London: Penguin Books, 1990), 76.
5. *Understanding and Managing High Blood Pressure*, American Heart Association and the American Stroke Association (Dallas: 2014), www.heart.org/idc/groups/heart-public/@ wcm/@hcm/documents/downloadable/ucm_461840.pdf.

ABOUT THE AUTHORS

CHRISTOPHER PAYNE

Chris is an economist with vast international experience in banking and finance. He began his career at Price-Waterhouse Coopers in London, where he qualified as a chartered accountant. At JPMorgan Chase & Co., he was vice president of Asian equities. He managed emerging-market equity funds at F&C Asset Management. As a senior economist at Bloomberg, he authored numerous studies on the Dodd-Frank Wall Street Reform and Consumer Protection Act, Basel III, and US monetary and fiscal policy. He was head of research at the Kuwait Institute of Banking Studies, where he authored papers for the country's leading financial institutions, including the Central Bank of Kuwait, on the future development of the nation's banking and financial system. He holds a bachelor's degree from Cambridge University, England, and master's and doctorate degrees from the London School of Economics. His previous book, *The Consumer, Credit and Neoliberalism: Governing the Modern Economy*, relates economic theory to monetary and banking policy in the United Kingdom and the United States leading up to the global financial crisis of 2008.

ROB BARNETT

Rob Barnett is a seasoned energy professional with over fifteen years' experience advising investors, policy makers, and executives at Fortune 500 companies. His areas of expertise include the political economy of fossil fuels, energy sector economics, environmental regulation, and the impact of government policy on energy investment decisions. Currently based in London, Barnett is a senior energy policy analyst at Bloomberg Intelligence. Before joining Bloomberg Intelligence, he was Bloomberg Government's senior energy economist in Washington, DC; and previously he was an associate director of climate change and clean energy at IHS Cambridge Energy Research Associates in Boston. He has authored numerous studies on climate change policy, coal regulations, and the future of the oil business. He holds a master's degree in economics from Boston University and undergraduate and master's degrees in electrical engineering from Clemson University.